Scotland and Britain

1830 - 1980

SAS Chalmers & Larry Cheyne

Hodder & Stoughton
LONDON SYDNEY AUCKLAND

ACKNOWLEDGEMENTS

· ·

The Publishers would like to thank the following for permission to reproduce copyright illustrations in this volume: Cover – "The U.C.S. – The Fight for the Right to Work" by Ken Currie, People's Palace, Glasgow Museums. Mary Evans Picture Library p.7; p.40. Fawcett Library/Mary Evans Picture Library p.70. New Lanark Conservation Trust p.10. Strathclyde Regional Archives p.26. The Mansell Collection p.11; p.19 right; p.27; p.30; p.33. The Hulton-Deutsch Collection p.12; p.13; p.19 left; p.25; p.41; p.47; p.52 lower; p.53 lower left; p.53 right; p.61 p.62 lower; p.64; p.65 p.72 both; p.77 right; p.78 left; p.83. Graham Collection, The Mitchell Library, Glasgow p.14. William Young Collection, The Mitchell Library, Glasgow p.37 left both. The Mitchell Library, Glasgow p.57. George Washington Wilson Collection, Aberdeen University Library p.16; p.18; p.51 right; p.75 right. Punch Publications p.21; p.23; p.35. Northamptonshire Libraries and Information Service p.29. The Illustrated London News Picture Library p.31. Mrs Barbara Linehan p.36 top. People's Palace (Glasgow Museums) p.36 bottom. The Annan Collection p.37 bottom right. Glasgow Golf Club p.38 lower. Reproduced by permission of The Imperial War Museum, London p.42 left; p.56. Topham p.42 right; p.43; p.49 right; p.63; p.75 left; p.108 both. Beamish North of England Open Air Museum p.44; p.85. The John Gorman Collection p.45 both; p.55. City of Aberdeen Library Services p.46 top; p.54 left. Glasgow University Archives p.46 bottom; p.76. BMIHT/Rover Group p.48; p.88; p.92 both. Aerofilms p.49 left both. The National Railway Museum p.50 top; p.51 top left. Scottish Record Office/British Railway Board p.51 top. United Distillers p.51 bottom left. Royal Scottish Automobile Club p.52 top. The Scotsman Publications Ltd p.53 top left; p.54 right; p.106; p.107 right. York City Archives p.22; p.58. Batsford Publications p.59. The Kobal Collection p.62 top. The Museum of London p.68; p.69 The British Library p.73. Department of Stills & Posters, The British Film Institute p.77. Aberdeen Journals p.78 right. Glasgow Herald p.89. Scottish Enterprise p.90. Northern Ireland Equal Opportunities Commission p.91. East Kilbride Development Corporation p.95. Express Newspapers p.96. Mike Abrahams/ Network p.98. David Low/Centre for the Study of Cartoon and Caricature, University of Kent at Canterbury p.100. Rex p.107.

The Publishers would also like to thank the following for permission to reproduce material in this volume: Extracts reproduced from *All Our Working Lives* by Peter Pagnamenta and Richard Overy with the permission of BBC Enterprises Limited; *Glasgow Herald* for the extracts dated from August 1990; The extract by Maggy Meade-King c *The Guardian*; HMSO for the extracts from *Britain Handbook*, compiled by the Central Office of Information, Crown copyright; the extracts from *Railways* by Richard Tames (1970) by permission of Oxford University Press. Every effort has been made to trace and acknowledge of copyright. The Publishers will be glad to make suitable arrangements with any copyright holders whom it has not been possible to contact.

The cover picture is Panel 7 of the People's Palace History paintings "The UCS – the fight for the right to work" by Ken Currie.

British Library Cataloguing in Publication Data
SAS Chalmers and Larry Cheyne
   Scotland and Britain: 1830-1980.
   – (Standard grade history)
   I. Title   II. Series

ISBN 0-340-54218-8

First published 1992

© 1992 SAS Chalmers and Larry Cheyne

Typeset by Litho Link Limited, Welshpool, Powys, Wales.
Printed in Great Britain for the educational publishing division of Hodder & Stoughton Ltd, Mill Road, Dunton Green, Sevenoaks, Kent by Thomson Litho Ltd, East Kilbride.

CONTENTS

• •

SERIES PREFACE

The books in this series are designed to present major historical themes, change, co-operation and conflict, people and power. Key ideas in British, European and World history derived from these themes provide the basis for the organisation of content. The books make use of different types of evidence – primary and secondary, written, statistical and pictorial. Users of the books are guided towards their own understanding of history, based on their individual abilities and interests, as each section (chapter) progresses from simpler statements of ideas and issues to a consideration and analysis of more detailed and complex evidence.

It is the hope of the authors that the books in the series will increase understanding of the chosen themes as well as enthusiasm for investigating people, actions and events in history. Those who use the books will be encouraged to decide for themselves about the evidence they contain and to have their own views of the past.

Graeme Coy.

● *A note on money*

The decimal system we use today began in 1971. This book uses old money. The table gives the equivalent value of old money today.

1 shilling	= 5 new pence
10 shillings	= 50 new pence
20 shillings	= £1.00
1 old penny (1d)	= 0.41 new pence

SECTION A

1830-80

1

SCOTLAND AND BRITAIN IN 1830

● *Society in 1830*

A Britain in 1830.

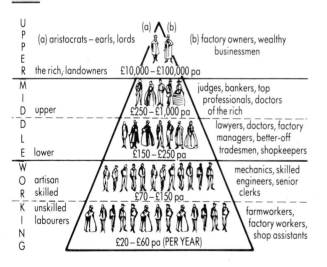

Britain in 1830 was a very different country from the one we live in today. The population was around 16 million, today it is over 55 million. It was also different because people were divided into classes according to their birth, wealth or job. Different classes kept very much to themselves and did not know much about how others lived. It was very difficult to move up in class because the landowners considered 'family breeding' to be very important and looked down on people who had made money from 'trade', although trade made most of Britain's wealth.

● *Growing Population*

In 1830 the number of people in Britain was increasing rapidly. This is shown in the table of official census figures.

B Census data.

Year	England	Scotland	Great Britain
1811	10,100,000	1,800,000	11,900,000
1831	13,900,000	2,300,000	16,200,000
1851	17,900,000	2,900,000	20,800,000
1871	22,700,000	3,300,000	26,000,000
1891	29,000,000	4,000,000	33,000,000
Increase	287%	222%	277%

This rise in population was caused by people having larger families (rising birth rate), living longer (falling death rate),

5

and more people coming to live in Britain (immigrating) than were leaving it (emigrating).

In 1801 only 25 per cent of the British people lived in towns but more and more were moving there in search of work. By 1851 54 per cent lived in towns and the number increased to 70 per cent by the end of the century.

?

1 Draw a pyramid like source A and place the five people below in their correct place in society:
   judge
   engineer
   factory owner
   factory worker
   earl

2 Write a sentence or two about each saying:
   a) what class they belong to,
   b) who earns most and who earns least,
   c) whom they look up to.

3 Why did the population of Scotland rise in the nineteenth century?

4 Draw two circles. Shade the first circle to show the percentage of people living in British towns in 1801 and the second to show the percentage living in towns at the end of the century.

*M*IGRATION

People moved to the towns for a variety of reasons.

C Taking Glasgow as the centre, there are persons who have come to it from . . .

within a circuit of 60 miles. My father originally came from the Lothians, and had been a country farmer; he was driven out by the improvements in farming, became a mechanic, and settled in Glasgow . . . When the cottagers were driven from their [jobs on the land], they first [moved to] villages, and then gradually moved to the large towns.

A report from an inhabitant of Glasgow in 1838.

D The coal and iron and textile industries (of Lanarkshire) were the magnets that attracted tens of thousands of immigrants in search of daily bread . . . With this expansion of Glasgow came the growth of the Irish population . . . The decline of the linen and woollen industries in the north of Ireland and the rise of the cotton industry in the west of Scotland . . . caused the flow of Irish towards the city.

J E Handley, The Irish in Scotland, *1947.*

By 1840 it was thought that one person in four living in Glasgow was Irish.

?

1 Describe the class system in Britain in 1830.

2 Explain why it would be almost impossible for an engineer to be accepted as an equal by a lord.

3 Was the population of England or Scotland rising more quickly in the nineteenth century? Give three possible reasons for the difference.

4 Use sources C and D to explain how and why
   a) Scots and
   b) Irish came to live in and around Glasgow.

5 Why is source C a good one for explaining the migration to the towns in the early nineteenth century?

2 PEOPLE AT WORK

● Agriculture

The Census of 1831 showed that farming was still the most common way of earning a living. In England, over one million families worked on the land. The food they produced fed most of the population. In Scotland also, agriculture was the most important industry in the country. Two thirds of the population worked for farmers for wages. Often wages were low. Labourers in the south of England earned as little as 7 shillings (35p) a week.

Hours of work were often long, and the work hard. This was true for men, working as skilled ploughmen or as labourers, and for women, both outdoors as dairy maids and indoors as farm servants.

In 1832 William Cobbett MP visited Scotland, and described the life of farm workers.

A Six days, from daylight to dark, these good and laborious people labour. A married man receives in money about four pounds for the year, He also gets oats, barley, peas and potatoes. He pays for his own fuel; he must find a woman to reap for twenty whole days in the harvest, as payment for the rent of his boothie. They never have wheat bread, nor beef nor mutton, though the land is covered with wheat and cattle.

The farm yards are, in fact, factories for making corn and meat, carried mainly by means of horses and machinery.

William Cobbett, A Tour of Scotland, 1833.

Farming was changing. More and more open fields were being enclosed. Farmers were becoming more willing to try new methods. New steam-powered machinery was appearing.

B Nearly every farm in the Lothians has its steam engine. In the county of Haddington, which contains about 200,000 acres, there were, in 1853, 185 steam engines.

An account from 1855.

C Farm labourers using a steam threshing machine.

The use of such machinery led to fewer jobs on the land. Wages stayed low, or even fell. More and more men left the land to look for jobs in the cities. Even city slums seemed better than working 12 or 14 hours a day, in all weathers, to live in a hut with no water or toilet, on a diet in which meat, or even cheese, was a little known luxury.

D Farm work was exhausting, looked down on, and grossly underpaid. It was dangerous; you were out in all weathers. Very few of those who managed to escape it returned of their own free will.

Harry Snell, farm worker.

?

1 Was farm work well paid? Give evidence from the sources to support your answer.

2 Why is Cobbett's *Tour of Scotland* (source A) a good source for finding out about life on the land at this time?

3 What shows that farming was important to people and the economy in the 1830s?

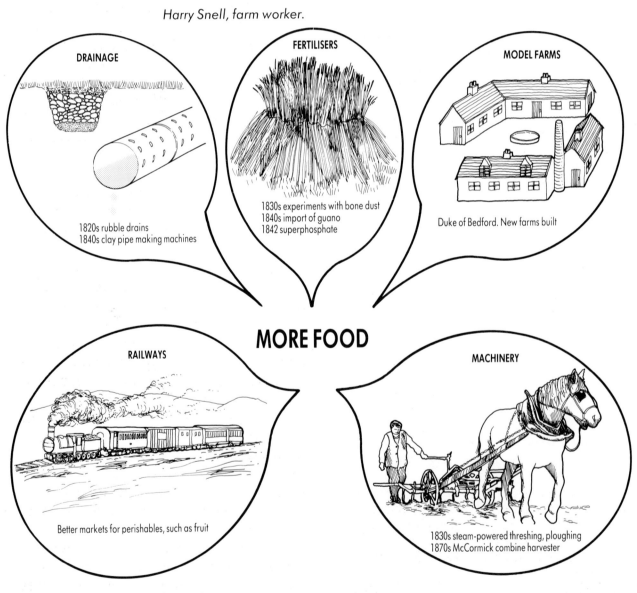

DRAINAGE

1820s rubble drains
1840s clay pipe making machines

FERTILISERS

1830s experiments with bone dust
1840s import of guano
1842 superphosphate

MODEL FARMS

Duke of Bedford. New farms built

MORE FOOD

RAILWAYS

Better markets for perishables, such as fruit

MACHINERY

1830s steam-powered threshing, ploughing
1870s McCormick combine harvester

E New methods of production.

CHANGES IN AGRICULTURE
1830-80

• •

This period has sometimes been called the 'Golden Age' of British agriculture. For farmers and landowners this was true. Food prices were generally high, and rents could be paid easily. Because of this, there was an incentive to produce more. Farmers adopted many new methods to increase production.

THE REPEAL OF THE CORN LAWS

• •

Corn Laws had been passed to protect British farming from imports of cheap foreign corn. They were very unpopular – poor people thought that they made bread dearer. Manufacturers thought they could sell more goods abroad if Britain bought food from other countries. In 1839 a group of Manchester industrialists formed the Anti-Corn Law League. They employed 12 full-time organisers; they printed pamphlets and distributed them by the new Penny Post. Their leaders, John Bright and Richard Cobden, were good orators, and even became MPs in 1843.

F We want free trade in corn, because we think it is just. We do not think it will injure the farmer. Neither do we think it will injure the farm labourer; we think it will increase his chances of employment. There will be a general rise in wages because of the rise in demand for labour. There will be more jobs for skilled men and labourers, clerks, shopmen and warehousemen. Finally, it will increase the government's revenue.

Part of a speech made by Richard Cobden in London, 1844.

The Conservative Government, led by Robert Peel and supported by Tory landowners, still refused to repeal the Corn Laws. However, in 1845 a terrible famine broke out in Ireland. Fearing a million deaths, Peel abandoned the Corn Laws.

British farmers were hardly affected by their repeal. The next 25 years were more prosperous than ever. But, in Ireland, one and a half million people starved, and as many more were forced to emigrate. For them, the repeal of the Corn Laws came too late. As well as the repeal of the Corn Laws, other legal obstacles to trade were removed as part of a Free Trade policy.

?

1 What arguments does Cobden give in source F for repealing the Corn Laws (free trade in corn)?

2 Was Cobden's view of the Corn Laws fair or biased? Give reasons to support your answer.

3 Do you think Peel was right to repeal the Corn Laws? Justify your answer.

4 Do you think that the period 1830-70 deserves the description the 'Golden Age' of British agriculture? Give reasons for your answer.

● *The Growth of Factories*

By 1830, big changes had begun to take place in the way goods were manufactured. The main reason for this was the rise in population. More people needed more clothes, more fuel and many other things.

As a result of this growth in demand, new ways of producing these goods were invented. In the eighteenth century most goods had been made in small workshops, or in people's homes. But in the cloth, or textile, industry there had been a series of inventions that changed this. New machines, such as the Mule, for spinning thread, and the Power Loom, for weaving cloth were now more common.

These machines were large and were driven by water or steam power. They were too large to fit into workers' homes. They were too expensive for most

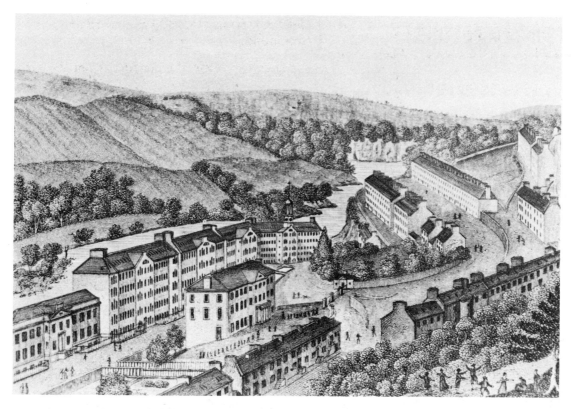

G New Lanark mills on the River Clyde.

workers to afford. So special factories were built to hold them. At first the factories used water power, and so were built near fast-flowing rivers. New Lanark, below, is an example of this.

Later factories were often built near coalfields, where they were near the fuel they needed. Factory owners built houses to rent to the workers, and opened shops to sell them food. They often paid higher wages to attract workers, but by today's standards these wages were low. One girl was paid 3s 7½d (17p) for a week of 112 hours! Working conditions in factories were often unpleasant. John Brown remembers what happened to Robert Blincoe, aged eight years, when he started work in a factory:

H The first task he was given was to pick up loose cotton, which fell on the floor. He set to work freely, although terrified by the whirling motion and noise of the machinery, but was soon affected by the dust and stench. He felt sick, and his back ached. But he was not allowed to sit down. He worked for 6½ hours without a rest.

In mills like those in Manchester, the heat is between 70 and 90 degrees Fahrenheit. [21 – 26 Centigrade.]

1 Why were factories built?

2 Were wages high or low? Explain your answer.

3 In what ways were factory conditions unpleasant?

4 What evidence is there that factory work was dangerous?

FACTORY REFORM IN TEXTILES

Many people were critical of factories.

I Thousands of our fellow-subjects, both male and female, are at this moment existing in a state of slavery. The factory system is necessary, but it is not necessarily an evil. It compels the kind-hearted master either to give up business, or to copy the cruel owners.

Richard Oastler, Tory MP, quoted in the Leeds Mercury, *1830.*

Pictures like the one below showed what conditions were like.

J Inside a textile factory.

Because of popular support for Oastler and others, the government set up a Royal Commission. Its Report, published in 1833, confirmed how bad conditions were. The government immediately passed a Factory Act. This limited the hours of work of women and children, and forbade them to work at night. Most importantly, it appointed four Inspectors to make sure the Act was obeyed. The Act only applied, however, to textile factories. Factory reformers had hoped that, without women and children to tend the machines, men's hours would be reduced.

K In the factory freedom comes to an end. The workman must be in the factory at half-past five. If he comes in a few minutes late, he is punished; if he comes in ten minutes late he is not allowed to enter until after breakfast, and thus loses a quarter of a day's wage. He must eat, drink and sleep at a word of command.

Friedrich Engels, The Condition of the Working Class in England, *1844.*

In 1844 another Factory Act was passed, but it still did not completely solve the problem. After another three years of campaigning by Lord Shaftesbury, the 1847 Factory Act limited hours of work for everyone in textile mills to ten a day.

In other industries, however, conditions did not improve.

L My parents were both labourers, working at brickmaking; twelve hours was a short day then. At six years old, I turned a rope-spinner's wheel from 6 am till 6 pm for 2s 6d (12p), whilst working as barber's lather boy till 11 pm for 1s (5p) a week. At fourteen I worked in a Birmingham munitions factory for 12 hour shifts, 18 hour shifts at weekends, pulling metal strips for the great rollers, and dropping bars into the pickling tubs, my hands scarred to the bone, my clothes eaten to rags by vitriol splashes. Many a time I have dreamt of the place, waking up in a cold sweat of fear.

Will Thorne, a trade union leader, born near Birmingham in 1857.

● Reform in Other Factories

Slowly the Factory Acts were extended to cover other industries. By 1867 all factories employing over 50 people were covered. In 1878 the Acts limited women in non-textile works to 60 hours a week; no child under 10 could be employed; and at last the law covered safety and ventilation.

❓

1 How far did Oastler and Engels agree about the effects of factories on workers? Support your answer with evidence from the sources.

2 Do you agree that the 1833 Factory Act was necessary? Justify your answer.

3 Why were later Factory Acts necessary?

● *Coal: the most important product*

Towards the end of the nineteenth century, Stanley Jevons, an economist, wrote: 'Coal stands above all other products in importance.' Output of coal rose rapidly. In 1830 output was about 30 million tons a year. By 1880 it was over 150 million tons. Likewise, the number of people employed in mining rose from 219,000 in 1851 to 503,900 in 1881. By that time, only agriculture employed more people.

In the 1830s working conditions in the mines were poor. After the Factory Act of 1833 was passed, Lord Shaftesbury persuaded parliament to set up an enquiry into conditions in the mines. In 1842 the Children's Employment Commission published its Report on the Collieries and Iron-works in the East of Scotland. The Commissioners talked to people working in the mines.

M Janet Cumming, 11 years old:
I work with my father and have done so for two years. Father starts at two in the morning; I start with the women at five and come up at five at night. I work all night on Fridays, and come up at twelve on Saturday.

I carry coal from the face to the pit-bottom. The weight is usually a hundredweight, and the distance between 50 and 80 yards. The roof is very low; I have to bend my back and legs, and the water often comes up to the calves of my legs. I have no liking for the work, but father makes me like it.

George Reid, 16 years old:
I pick coal at the coal face. I have done this for six years. The seam is 26 inches high and when I pick I have to twist myself up. It is horrible sore work; none ever come up for meals. Pieces of bread are taken down. Six of the family work with father below; when work is good he takes away £1 to £1.25 a week.

Jane Watson, age 40:
I have worked underground for 33 years. I have had nine children and two dead born, which was due to the work. I have always had to work till the birth, and return after 10 or 12 days.

It is only horse-work, and ruins the women; it makes them old at 40. Women get so weak that they are forced to take the little ones down to help them, even children of six years old.

Report on the Collieries and Iron-works in the East of Scotland.

They also published drawings of conditions underground, like these.

N Working in the coal mines.

As a result of the evidence, the Mines Act was passed in 1842. It forbade women and children under 10 to work underground. Inspectors were appointed to make sure it was obeyed.

?

Imagine you worked in a coal mine in 1842.

1 Give your evidence to the Commission about your work. Mention ● the work you did
● the hours you worked
● the conditions you worked in
● whether or not you liked the work (Give your reasons).

2 Say whether or not you were happy with the 1842 Mines Act. (Again, give your reasons.)

CHANGES IN MINING 1830-80

● The Demand for Coal

The rising demand for coal to drive steam-powered machinery in the cotton industry had caused output of coal to double between 1815 and 1830. As the century progressed, demand from other industries increased. Iron needed about 4 tons of coal to produce 1 ton of pure iron. Twenty-five per cent of all coal was used in metal manufacturing. Scotland was the fastest growing iron producer; it produced 5 per cent of Britain's iron in 1820, but 20 per cent by 1851. Transport was another expanding market. The years up to 1880 were the growth years of the railway; by then steam ships were also in greater use. To meet this ever growing demand for coal, pits got deeper and larger

P Miners having a break. This photograph was taken around 1950.

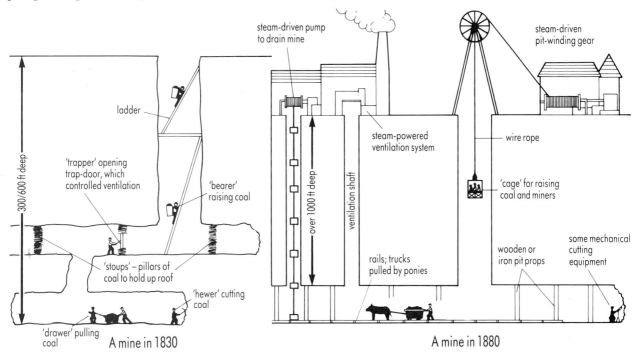

O Changes in coal mining between 1830 and 1880.

Despite these changes, mining was still an unpleasant, poorly-paid and dangerous job. While men were paid between 12p and 25p a day, women barely got half that. Accidents were common. Every five hours a miner was killed; every two minutes one was injured. Yet the Duke of Hamilton drew royalties of £100,000 a year from the coal dug beneath 'his' earth.

?

1   Why did output of coal grow so rapidly in this period? Give three reasons.

2   How much did working conditions in the mines change between 1830 and 1880?

● *Railways 1830-80*

Building the railways

In 1825 a group of Manchester factory owners raised £400,000 to build a railway between Liverpool and Manchester. They said it would cut the cost of transport by at least one third. After the railway opened in 1830, they found:

Q Coaches could only carry 688 persons per day; the railway carried an average of 1070 per day. The coach fare was 50p inside and 25p outside; by railway it is 25p inside and 17½p outside. The time by coach was four hours; by railway it is one hour and three quarters. Goods are delivered in Manchester the same day from Liverpool. By canal they were never delivered before the third day.

Annual Register, 1832.

The clear advantages of railways made other groups hurry to raise money to build them. Gangs of labourers known as 'navvies' were hired to do the hard manual work.

R Rude, rugged and uncultivated, they are a class and a community by themselves; rough in morals and manners; displaying an unbending vigour and an independent bearing; undisciplined; unable to read and unwilling to be taught; impetuous, impulsive and brute-like, herding together like beasts of the field.

J R Francis, History of the English Railway, *1851.*

J R Francis also described the way they lived:

S They earned high wages, and spent them. Many of them lived in a drunken state until their money was spent, and they were forced to look for work again. They made their houses where they got their work. Some slept in huts of damp turf, too low to stand up in; the roof was small sticks, covered with straw. It mattered not to them that the rain beat through the roof, and that winds swept through the holes.

The work was hard and dangerous. Using a pick and shovel, and sometimes gunpowder, each man shifted 20 tons of earth a day. Tunnelling was especially dangerous, with explosions and cave-ins claiming the lives of many.

T Digging Bishopton Cutting, near Paisley, 1842.

?

1 What four advantages did railways have, according to the Annual Register? (Source Q.)

2 Find four words or phrases (from source R) that show that J R Francis did not approve of the navvies.

3 What dangers did navvies face in their work?

*T*HE GROWTH OF THE RAILWAY SYSTEM

• •

One problem faced by the railway companies was buying the land they needed.

U Scarcely any instance is known of a reasonable price being asked for the portion required by the railway proprietors. One spirit pervades all – a determination to extort as much as they can. In dealing with railways, men think themselves entitled to cheat without restraint.

Chambers' Edinburgh Review, 1838.

Many lines were promoted by local businessmen, largely to gain access to markets and raw materials. Others were promoted by fraudsters, to cheat people of their money. Many small companies went bankrupt after the 'Railway Mania' of 1844-5.

Despite this, the Scottish Railway system expanded, as shown in the map opposite.

A similar expansion took place in many parts of Britain.

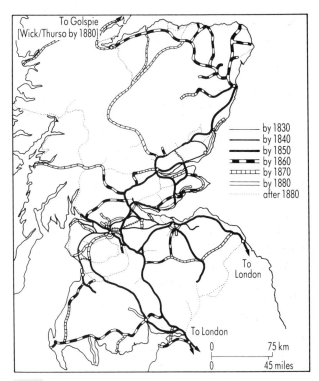

V The expansion of Scottish Railways, 1830-80.

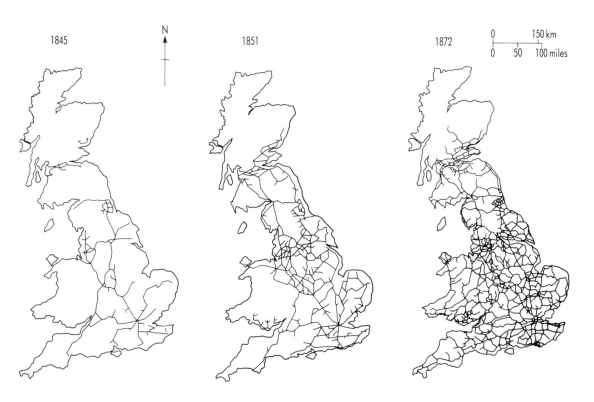

W The railway network in Britain in 1845, 1851 and 1872.

This expansion required some major engineering works, such as the Tay Bridge, opened in June 1878.

X Tay Bridge.

Because of the large sums of money involved, and the possible danger to life and limb, the government felt forced to take some control. It passed a series of Acts to regulate the railways.

1840 Railway Regulating Act: Railways were put under the control of the Board of Trade, who appointed inspectors who had access to reports on traffic, charges and safety.

1844 Railway Act: This had three main parts:
a) Each company had to run 'Parliamentary Trains' daily over each line, stopping at each station, at a minimum speed of 12 mph.
b) The fare for 3rd class passengers was 1d per mile.
c) All carriages had to have doors, seats and windows.

1845 Gauge Act: All new railways had to be Standard Gauge (4ft 8½ins between the tracks).

1854 Railway and Canal Traffic Act: Railways were not to favour one customer with cheaper charges than another.

1873 Regulation of Railways Act: A commission was set up to decide on railway amalgamations and charges for cargoes.

?

1 What effect did the attitude of landowners have on the cost of building railways? (Source U.)

2 Describe the growth of the Scottish railway system, both before and after 1840.

3 Which area(s) of Britain had fewest railways by 1872?

4 Study the list of Acts.
Then copy and complete the table below, by putting a tick in each box to show what each Act tried to control.
One example, the 1845 Gauge Act, is done for you.

	1840 Act	1844 Act	1845 Act	1854 Act	1873 Act
Safety/ Comfort					
Traffic/ Charges					
Technical Problems			✔		

THE BENEFITS OF RAILWAYS
. . . .

Thomas Creevey travelled on the Liverpool & Manchester Railway in 1830:

Y I had the satisfaction, for I can't call it pleasure, of taking a trip of five miles, at twenty miles an hour. It is really flying, and it is impossible to forget instant death coming to all if the least accident happens; It gave me a headache which has not yet left me.

Seven years later, Greville travelled from Birmingham to Liverpool:

Z At first I felt nervous and being run away with. But a sense of security soon came, and the speed was delightful. The view was a continually changing panorama. All other travelling is irksome and tedious by comparison.

Some passengers did complain of the lack of comfort on the early third class trains. But, as was commented in 1844:

AA The shabby rich, by using these trains, have only themselves to blame for being uncomfortable. We have been astounded to hear that men worth many thousands of pounds have used third class carriages on the Greenock Railway; some have even brought stools to sit on in these carriages.

Chambers' Edinburgh Review, 1844.

The 1844 Railway Act ensured that all carriages had to have seats, doors and windows; by the 1880s, the wealthy could hire private carriages, with a luggage compartment, private saloon, lavatory, pantry and a compartment for servants.

THE RESULTS OF THE RAILWAYS
. . . .

As early as 1832, industries soon grew up near the railways, as this map shows.

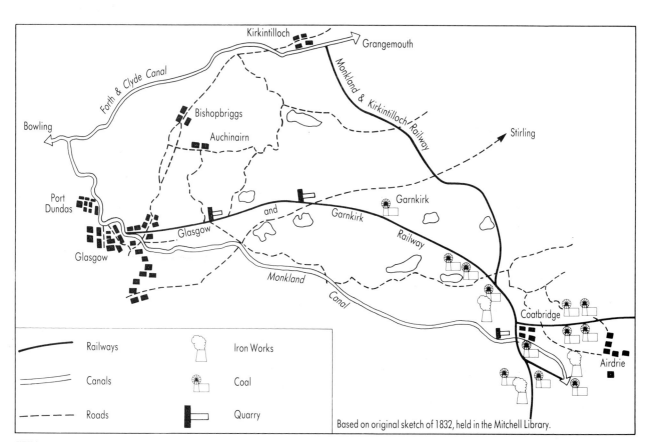

BB Transport in the 1830s, north and east of Glasgow.

The great railway builder, Robert Stephenson, made this speech to the Institution of Civil Engineers in January 1856:

CC The railways employ 90,400 officers and servants, while the engines consume annually two million tons of coal. In 1854, 111 million passengers were carried, each travelling an average of 12 miles.

The wear and tear is great. 20,000 tons of iron require to be replaced annually; 300,000 trees are annually felled to replace perished sleepers.

The postal facilities afforded by the railways are very great. Every Friday night, eight or ten vans are required to transport the weekly papers on the North Western Railway alone. Government papers would not be printed, for only the railways can transport them.

Robert Stephenson, 1856.

He could also have mentioned the growth of holiday resorts, like Brighton or Ayr, or the growth of desirable suburbs near the main cities, from which the wealthy commuted. He could have mentioned the growth of railway towns, like Crewe or Kilmarnock, or the growth of exports of railway goods – by the end of the century, the Springburn district of Glasgow alone made one quarter of the world's locomotives. Areas such as the Highlands were opened to tourism.

DD Lochawe Station and Hotel (1880).

1 Which traveller, Creevey or Greville, did not enjoy rail travel? Why did he not enjoy it?

2 What evidence is there that Chambers' Edinburgh Review did not approve of rich people travelling third class?

3 Describe how passenger comfort had improved by 1880.

Activity
Get into groups of about four. Read these pages about the growth of railways. Then, under each of the headings below, make lists of the effects that the coming of the railways had. You are given an example under each heading to start you off.

● *Jobs which were created on the railways*
Signalmen

● *Industries which could sell their products to the railways*
Clock-makers (for time-keeping)

● *Industries which could sell their products all over Britain*
Slate quarries

● *Types of town which grew as a result of the railways*
Dormitory towns (for commuters)

● *People/Industries which suffered as more people went by rail*
Private road companies (Turnpikes)

In the opinion of your group, did more people benefit or suffer from the growth of the railways?

HOME AND HEALTH

● *Housing*

A family's standard of living, how well off it is, is decided by the amount of money they have each week and how they spend it. In 1830 upper and middle-class people lived in comfortable homes with many luxuries and servants to look after them.

A A room in a Victorian middle-class home.

The working classes were not so lucky. They had to live near their work, often in a 'tied' house, that is one owned by their employer. If they lost their jobs they would be evicted from their homes.

This description of a country cottage was printed in the *Morning Chronicle* in 1850.

B The length is not above 15 feet, its width 10-12 . . . the walls wet . . . there are 2 rooms . . . one below and the other above. In the fireplace . . . a small wood fire, over which hangs a pot . . . At one corner a small rickety table . . . 3 old chairs and a stool or two. There is but one room (for sleeping) and we counted nine in the family. The beds are large sacks

filled with chaff . . . the clothes worn by the parents in the daytime make the main covering of the children by night.

Morning Chronicle, 1850.

But townsfolk were just as badly off, as shown by this drawing of a home in the early nineteenth century.

A one-room home.

C Urban overcrowding: a one-room family.

● *Disease*

Houses were very poor in both country and town but townspeople were worse off because so many families were crowded together. This helped disease spread more easily. The overcrowding, lack of drains and having between 50 and 200 people sharing dry toilets caused the rapid spread of killer diseases such as cholera.

Disease	Causes	Symptoms	Results
cholera	tiny bacteria in water	cramps, diarrhoea, sickness, turn blue	coma and death in 50 per cent of cases
typhoid	bad water and food	fever, diarrhoea, reddish rash	possible death
typhus	body lice, dirty houses, overcrowding	fever, headaches, rose-coloured rash	possible death
consumption/ tuberculosis	overcrowding, bad diet, poor ventilation	cough, spit blood, fever, waste away	death death

Only when many thousands, poor and rich, died in epidemics did the government start to take notice. In 1842 the Report on the Sanitary Conditions of the Labouring Population made recommendations, as follows:

D The most important things needed are drains, removing rubbish from streets, and purer water. There should be improved sewers and drains and a medical officer of health (doctor) should be put in charge of each district.

Report on the Sanitary Conditions of the Labouring Population, 1842.

The Public Health Act 1848 gave towns powers to set up Boards of Health to make sure all new houses had drains and lavatories and were supplied with pure water. Although some towns did try to make improvements, a report of 1869 said many were as bad as they had been in 1830.

1   What two things decide if a family has a good standard of living?

2   Imagine you are going to investigate the standard of living of people from the past. Make up at least four questions you need to ask about their lives.

3   Compare homes in the country and in the town. Look at sources B and C and fill out the chart below. Leave blanks if you do not have the information.

Housing and Health

Information required	Country	Town
Number of people Number of rooms Size of rooms State of repair Method of lighting Method of cooking		

4   Choose the house in either the country or the town.
    a) What diseases might the family catch?
    b) Explain why.
    c) Find two reasons why families stayed in such bad conditions.

5   Study the table of killer diseases and the recommendations of the 1842 Report. (Source D.) Choose two recommendations and explain for *each*:
    a) What disease(s) it would fight.
    b) How it would help reduce the number of people killed.

6   What reforms had been passed by 1850?

UNDERSTANDING DISEASE

Doctors in the early nineteenth century did not know about germs and bacteria and, when the cholera epidemic of 1831-3 killed 10,000 Scots, they blamed it on 'miasmas' or 'effluvia', that is, smells floating around in the air. They might not know the cause but their work showed them the sort of conditions where disease flourished.

E Another defect in some parts of Edinburgh is the great size . . . of the houses (some 10 storeys), with common stairs, sometimes as filthy as the streets. The chance of cleanliness is lessened by the labour of carrying up . . . water . . . I may state that with Mr Chadwick . . . the police superindentent and others, we visited a house at the back of the Canongate . . . occupied by families of the labouring classes. A widow of respectable appearance, who answered some of our questions, occupied a room above . . . a pigsty. . . On the occasion of the dungheap being removed from the pigsty, a daughter and a niece, were made ill by the effluvia from below, and both died.

Report on the Sanitary Conditions of the Labouring Population, 1842.

The population of Airdrie, a weaving town in the Lanarkshire coalfields, increased from 5,000-14,000 between 1821 and 1846, with resulting problems of water supply. In 1846 towns in general had an average of seven grains of harmful substances per gallon of drinking water, but an analysis in Airdrie in 1849 showed the following:

F

Source of water	Total Amount in grains of harmful matter in 1 gallon	Substances found in water
Town well	56	iron
County jail	84	
National bank	134	natural waste, iron
Clarkston pit	46	iron
Clarkston spring	8	natural waste, iron
Rawyards spring	22	iron

G This is a cartoon from the magazine *Punch* in the 1850s which draws attention to pollution in the River Thames.

IMPROVEMENTS IN HEALTH AND HOUSING

After the 1869 report said many towns were as unhealthy as they had been in the 1830s, the Public Health Acts of 1872/5 tried to establish minimum conditions throughout Britain.

- Local councils had to lay sewers, drains and pavements, provide street cleansing and provide towns with street lighting and fire services.
- Medical Officers of Health were appointed to deal with infections and take measures to cope with disease and stop it spreading.
- Sanitary inspectors not only made sure that streets and buildings were kept clean, they could also seize contaminated food and destroy it.
- Councils could provide water and lavatories where necessary and they could build baths and wash-houses to help people keep clean.

These improvements were more difficult to carry out in the older parts of towns so the Artisans' Dwelling Act of 1875, which allowed councils to take over and demolish slum areas, was very important. It gave councils powers they could use when they found money for improvements.

H A by-law terrace. These houses are typical examples of those built in the late nineteenth century.

1 Use sources, A, B and C to show at least four ways middle-class housing was more comfortable than working-class housing.

2 What were the main causes of disease in the middle of the nineteenth century?

3 Study source E.
a) Make a table showing the causes of disease mentioned and say which diseases are likely to occur.
b) Explain why this is a useful source for telling us about the reasons for ill-health in the cities.

4 Study source F.
a) Do you think it was healthy to drink water in Airdrie? Give reasons for your answer.
b) Why do you think it was so bad?

5 Cartoons often exaggerate because they are trying to win people over to their viewpoint. How can you tell source E is exaggerating?

6 **Research**
Use materials from your class and school library to find out about one of the cholera epidemics between 1831 and 1854. Write a short paragraph explaining how local authorities dealt with it.

7 What improvements were made to the sanitation of towns after 1875?

8 Why was the appointment of Medical Officers of Health and Sanitary Inspectors important?

9 How far do you think the recommendations of 1842 (source D) had been achieved by 1880?

STANDARD OF LIVING AND POVERTY

● *Food for the Family*

Before 1850 almost three-quarters of a poor family's wages were likely to be spent on food. This tended to be dull and boring as shown by this account of Manchester cotton workers in 1833.

A Their main food is potatoes and wheaten bread, washed down by tea or coffee. Meal (oatmeal) is eaten, either baked into cakes or boiled up with water, making a nourishing porridge which is easily digested and cooked. Animal food makes a very small part of their diet, and what they eat is often of poor quality. Fish is sometimes bought, usually herrings. Because these are salted they are difficult to digest. Eggs too make some part of their diet. The main food, however, is tea and bread.

Mrs Gaskell, The Manufacturing Population of England, *1833.*

Often, wives were also out working and did not have much time to cook. Bacon was often added to potatoes. Sometimes children only had bacon grease to eat, while father ate the bacon. Many families could only afford to eat meat at Christmas or Easter and had to get the baker to cook it in his oven.

They bought food in small amounts from a local shopkeeper who often tried to make more money by adulterating it, that is, adding other materials so he could make a bigger profit.

Source B shows us the effects of this.

THE USE OF ADULTERATION.

Little Girl. "IF YOU PLEASE, SIR, MOTHER SAYS, WILL YOU LET HER HAVE A QUARTER OF A POUND OF YOUR BEST TEA TO KILL THE RATS WITH, AND A OUNCE OF CHOCOLATE AS WOULD GET RID OF THE BLACK BEADLES?"

B A cartoon from *Punch*, 1855.

?

1 Draw a circle and mark in it the part of their wages workers before 1850 spent on food, and what was left for everything else.

2 Write out a day's menu for a cotton worker's family.
Breakfast:
Dinner: (noon)
Supper: (evening)

3 Do you think this is a healthy diet? Explain your answer by thinking of the foods they do not eat.

● *Making Ends Meet*

This is an account of how a farm labourer spent his wages.

C Weekly budget of Robert Crick, farm labourer, Lavenham, Suffolk, c. 1842

		Earnings
Robert Crick	(42 yrs)	9s 0d
Wife	(40 ″)	9d
Boy	(12 ″)	2s 0d
″	(11 ″)	1s 0d
″	(8 ″)	1s 0d
Girl	(6 ″)	—
Boy	(4 ″)	—
		13s 9d

	Expenditure
Bread	9s 0d
Potatoes	1s 0d
Rent	1s 2d
Tea	2d
Sugar	3½d
Soap	3d
Blue	½d
Thread etc.	2d
Candles	3d
Salt	½d
Coal and wood	9d
Butter	4½d
Cheese	3d
	13s 9d

Reports on the Employment of Women and Children in Agriculture, Parliamentary Papers, 1843.

Although factory workers were better paid, workers in old, declining industries like handloom weaving, suffered badly as this letter shows. It was written to the Duke of Hamilton by one of his estate officials.

D   Hamilton 18th Sept. 1826

Sir,

Upon an average a man's earnings will not exceed 1 shilling per day at the weaving working 14 hours and in many cases (he) will have three children and upwards. This sum only allows each member of the family one half *peck* of meal each, which amounts to 3 shillings and 11 pence halfpenny; 1 shilling 1 penny halfpenny for potatoes . . . for two . . . herrings 5 pence, 1.5 pence for salt.

In my opinion it would take one half more to keep them living. Nothing is allowed here for house rent, fire nor clothing. What becomes of them in the winter, God only knows.

POVERTY AND THE POOR LAW

• •

In the eighteenth century the 'kirk' or church of each Scottish parish looked after its own poor – the old or families whose wage earner was sick or out of work.

By the beginning of the nineteenth century towns and cities were growing larger, industry and jobs were changing and voluntary help was not enough. Many parishes brought in a special tax called 'the poor rate'. The better-off people who paid it complained that this encouraged laziness because people would not look for work if they were given money.

Paisley was a town of over 60,000 people working mainly in the textile industry. In 1843 a trade slump made over half the businesses bankrupt and over 15,000 unemployed. When the starving people had sold all they owned they had to rely on charities. The Prime Minister, Sir Robert Peel, and the Cabinet gave £2,000 of their own money to help them and prevent revolution. A Poor Law Commission was set up in Scotland that year. As a result, this new law was passed.

E   Scottish Poor Law Act 1845
1 A Central Board was appointed to supervise from Edinburgh.
2 Each parish had to set up a 'Parochial Board' to care for the poor.
3 The Parochial Board was given power to charge a poor rate from local people.
4 The Boards appointed inspectors to check on the poor who asked for help.
5 Inspectors could give:
   Outdoor Relief – a sum of money to help over a short period of time.
   Indoor Relief – put people in the poorhouse.
6 People entitled to receive help were the unhealthy, young, old and the physically or mentally handicapped. The unemployed still had to depend on charity.

Inspectors preferred to give indoor relief as it was cheaper and poor conditions discouraged people from applying unless they were desperate. In the poorhouses there were separate blocks for men, women and children. Where possible, people were given unpleasant work to do.

?

1 What was the 'poor rate'?

2 Why did better-off people object to it?

3 a) Who was in charge of helping the poor after 1845?
   b) Where did they send poor people?
   c) Explain why you would not like to be sent to a place like source F.

F   The Poorhouse.

POORHOUSE CONDITIONS

Those entering the poorhouse were bathed, put in uniform, medically examined and placed in probationary wards until it was decided what kind of work they could do and what sort of character they had. Those who were not healthy were put in the sick ward and the quiet and well-behaved in the healthy ward. Anyone else was sent to the 'Test Department' where there was strict discipline, hard work and harsh punishment – usually a cut in food or solitary confinement. Conditions were deliberately harsh to discourage idlers, or those who had families to help support them. The following sources are from poor law records of two cases from Douglas in Lanarkshire.

G *Name:* Margaret Park, single, aged 65
Occupation: domestic servant
Dependants: none
Information: Son Andrew aged 40, single miner, is in infirmary. She wishes relief until Andrew comes home.
Inspector's decision: offered poorhouse.
Decision of Parochial Board: outdoor relief at 1s 6d per week.

Applications for poor relief to Douglas Parish, 1881.

H *Name:* Agnes Dick, single, 24
Occupation: farm servant
Dependants: James Dick, aged 2
Information: Agnes, is expecting her second child, and has come to stay with her sister who seeks relief for her.

Inspector's decision: offered poorhouse.
Decision of Parochial Board: relief in poorhouse.

Applications for poor relief to Douglas Parish, 1881.

?

1 Study what happened in Paisley in 1843. Were the people who needed help there 'too lazy to work'? Explain your answer.

2 Why was the 1845 Poor Law Act needed to organise poor relief in Scotland?

3 a) Which groups of people were entitled to help?
   b) Who was not entitled to help?
   c) Do you think this was fair? Give reasons for your answer.

4 What were the four categories of inmate in Scottish poorhouses?

5 Describe the treatment given to those in the 'Test Department'. Explain why they were treated in this way.

6 Study the two cases from Douglas. Why do you think the two women were treated differently?

7 **Role Play**
   Make up a conversation between the inspector and either Margaret Park or Agnes Dick.

I Foresthall Hospital. This used to be Barnhill Workhouse.

5 EDUCATION

● *Schools 1830-80*

In 1800 Scotland had the best system of education in the world. As far back as 1599 the Church of Scotland had tried to set up a school in each parish. All local children, up to the age of 11, were taught to read, write and count. This system still existed in 1830. As these extracts show, the standard of education varied:

A A small boy, who appeared to be in charge for the moment, said this was the day that the children paid their fees, and the master was in the shop next door. I found him combining penmanship with porter, and Geography with Glenlivet.

Census taker in Glasgow.

B I went to the village school in Kilmaurs, from 9am till 4pm, with an hour off to eat my piece in the school shed. The children of the poor were probably as well educated as those of the wealthy in basic subjects like reading, writing and arithmetic.

John Boyd Orr.

As towns grew, however, few children there got any education at all. Others, like David Livingstone, taught themselves:

C At the age of ten I was put into the factory as a piecer. My reading while at work was carried on by placing the book in a portion of the spinning jenny, so that I could catch sentence after sentence as I passed.

David Livingstone.

Even in private fee-paying schools the quality of education could be poor.

D This cartoon was drawn in 1839.

In 1837, a government enquiry reported on the state of education in the towns:

E We took evidence on the state of Education in the large manufacturing and seaport towns, where the population has rapidly increased in the present century. Our main findings are:
1. The education given to working class children is very poor indeed.
2. Very few of these children [about one in eight] get any education at all.
3. Government action is necessary to improve the situation.

Report of the Select Committee of 1837: Education in Large Towns.

It was not until the Education Acts of 1870 (England and Wales) and 1872 (Scotland) that the government made any major changes. These Acts allowed ratepayers to elect School Boards for their local area. The Boards were responsible for building schools, maintaining them, and employing teachers; they could also pay the fees of children whose parents were poor. And attendance was compulsory – all children had to go to school, up to the age of 13.

?

1 In what way(s) was Orr's school better than the one in Glasgow? (Source B.)

2 Describe how David Livingstone was educated. (Source C.)

2 In which areas did the 1837 enquiry find education was poorest?

4 What powers did School Boards have?

DIFFERENT TYPES OF SCHOOLS 1830-80

• •

The social class of a child largely decided the type of education a child received. Dawson and Wall describe the education of a wealthy (male) child:

F Rich or middle class parents would engage a private tutor for their children, or send them to one of the old Grammar Schools. The very rich might send them to one of the nine great Public [private] schools. Education for the well-to-do consisted almost entirely of Latin Grammar, with Greek for the brighter pupils in the better schools. This Classical background was thought to be indispensible for a gentleman, who could use it to develop an interest in language, politics or philosophy.

Dawson and Wall, Education, 1969.

There were several types of schools for the poorer classes in the cities, where there were no parish schools. One of the earliest was Sunday school, where children who worked during the week were taught Bible study, and, in the process, reading. Other working children attended factory schools, which were held after working hours in the factory. There, teachers, often ministers, taught classes of up to 100, of varying ages, the three R's (Reading, Writing and 'Rithmetic). After a day at work, pupils often found it hard to concentrate.

There were also day schools of various types. Here Dawson and Wall describe one type:

G The worst type were the 'Dame's Schools'. They were little more than a means by which elderly spinsters or widows could earn a little money by taking children into their homes during the day. The children learnt very little and such schools were really only child-minding centres.

Dawson and Wall, Education, 1969.

Other schools were set up by religious bodies, such as the Episcopalian and Roman Catholic Churches. They, and the parish schools, increasingly used the 'monitorial' system to cope with the large classes in city schools. Here Joseph Lancaster describes the system:

H My school is attended by 300 scholars. The whole system of tuition is almost entirely conducted by boys. The school is divided into classes, to each of these a lad is appointed as monitor: he is responsible for the morals, improvement, good order, and cleanliness of the whole class. It is his duty to make a daily, weekly and monthly report of progress, specifying the number of lessons performed, boys present, absent etc. They also have to train other lads as assistants, to replace them when they leave. Everyone envies the monitors; we pay them.

Joseph Lancaster, Improvements in Education, 1803.

In this way, one teacher could supervise the teaching of a large number of pupils, as the picture on page 29 shows:

THE PATRON OF EDUCATION, AND FRIEND OF THE POOR.

The teaching methods in such schools are described in this teaching manual:

I Writing on Paper

When the girls have learned to write freely on slate, they are allowed to write also on copybooks. A monitor is appointed to each class. Each pupil collects her book, but remains standing. The command is then given by the monitor; 'Lay down books', 'Sit', 'Open books', 'Begin'. They are not allowed to write more than five lines. Each monitor then goes from girl to girl, pointing out defects by comparing it with the copy slip. At the command 'Show books', the mistress inspects. The monitor then says 'Lay down books', 'Shut books' and the books are collected in.

Manual of Teaching of the British and Foreign School Society.

J The monitor system.

?

1   How were the children of the well-to-do taught?

2   What evidence is there that Dawson and Wall did not think much of the 'Dame schools'?

3   What were the duties of a monitor?

Ask your teacher to conduct a lesson using the 'monitorial system'.

4   What are the differences compared to a lesson today?

5   Which system do you prefer? Give reasons to support your answer.

6 MEN OF POWER . . . PEOPLE WITHOUT IT

● *Men of Power in 1830*

As we have already seen, many working-class people in Britain lived in slums and worked long hours for wages so low they could barely survive. Why did they not improve things?

In any country, the people who have power are those who make the laws, control the army and police and can enforce obedience. This power belongs to the government. Britain in 1830 was governed by the king and parliament. Laws were passed when a majority of MPs in the House of Commons and the members of the House of Lords agreed. They then received the king's signature or assent.

The majority of men in both the House of Commons and House of Lords were landowners and passed laws to suit themselves. The people who elected MPs were either landowners, tenant farmers or businessmen. In Scotland, with a population of more than 2 million, only 4,289 had the right to vote.

Reform of government was needed. After a long hard struggle a Parliamentary Reform Act was passed in 1832.

A Results of the 1832 Reform Act.

1. 22 towns gained 2 seats   = 44
    20 towns gained 1 seat   = 20
    Extra seats for English counties = 65
    Extra seats for Scotland   = 8
    Extra seats for Ireland   = 5
2. Voters in town = pay yearly rent of £10
    Voters in county = 40 shilling freeholder, £10 long leaseholders, £50 short leaseholders
3. Population of Britain = 24,000,000
    Voters before 1832 Act = 435,000
    Voters after 1832 Act = 652,000
    Only 1 man in 7 (no women) had the vote.
4. Method of voting – saying openly.

In the reformed parliament the middle class and factory owners had more say.

B The House of Commons in 1834.

● Chartism

The working-class people had taken part in marches and riots during the struggle to win reform but the new parliament only seemed to make life more difficult for them. The 1833 Factory Act stopped children under eight-years-old working in textile factories but did nothing to reduce the hours their parents had to work. In 1834 the new Poor Law forced people into the dreaded workhouse. That same year six farm labourers from Tolpuddle in Dorset were transported to Australia when they joined a union to stop their wages being cut. In 1838 there was a trade slump and people were thrown out of work.

The educated workers realised that improved living and working conditions would only come about if the working class had political power. Thus the Chartist movement began in the mid-1830s.

Chartists wanted six reforms;
- the vote for all adult men
- secret voting
- men should not need to own land to become MPs
- MPs should be paid a wage
- all constituencies should have around the same number of voters
- parliament should be elected every year.

A petition demanding these reforms was sent to parliament in 1839. When parliament turned it down, disappointed Chartists turned to violence. People were shot at Newport in Wales and the government imprisoned 500 Chartist leaders.

The movement split into two with William Lovett and the 'moral force' group wanting to use peaceful methods, while Feargus O'Connor's 'physical force' Chartists wanted to use violence to force reform.

In 1842, during another slump, a second petition was presented – and ignored. There were strikes where the workers took the 'plugs' from the steam boilers.

C This picture from the *Illustrated London News* shows Chartists attacking the workhouse in Stockport and giving away bread they have taken from it.

Middle-class people were frightened by the violence and even when a third petition, said to have six million names on it, was presented in 1848 it was turned down. It had many forged names on it, for example, the Duke of Wellington and Queen Victoria.

The movement died away because it had asked for too much, was badly led, violent and was short of money.

It was 1867 before the vote was given to male householders in the boroughs and 1884 before it was given to male householders in the country.

?

1 Why is it true to say landowners had most power in Britain before 1832?

2 Give three ways conditions for working-class people grew worse in the 1830s.

3 Look at the six aims of the Chartists. Copy them out and, from the list below, choose the reason which fits with each aim.
 — so a few people could not elect an MP.
 — because it stopped working men becoming MPs.
 — so workers had a say in electing MPs.
 — so workers could afford to become MPs.
 — so parliament would have to do as the people wanted.
 — to stop employers and landlords telling people for whom they should vote.

4 In what ways is source C useful for showing us about Chartism? (Causes, supporters, methods.)

5 Why did the movement fail?

WHY REFORM WAS SO SLOW

At the time, the 1832 Reform Act was seen as a great change. This is what was said about it. The first account is from William Cobbett, who wanted Radical reform; the second is from the Duke of Wellington, the Prime Minister who fought against the Act.

D (i) Every sensible man sees that the Reform Bill is the commencement of a mighty revolution.

(ii) The revolution is made, power is transferred from one class of society, the gentlemen of England, to another class of society, the shopkeeper.

Wellington was wrong; the landowners kept the real power for more than 50 years after the Reform Act.

The failure of the Chartists came about not only because of their own weaknesses and the

opposition of the authorities but also because better living standards after 1843 turned the working class away from the movement. However, the fact Britain was changing did in fact help bring about the reforms the Chartists had wanted. W.E. Gladstone, the Liberal leader, made the following speech in parliament.

E Since 1832 religious influences, the civilising and training powers of education have been brought to the mass of the people. Newspapers are circulated by the million giving a new interest in public affairs. The self-improving powers of the working community . . . the Working Men's Free Libraries and Institutes . . . there are now 650,000 depositors in the Post Office Savings banks . . . What is the meaning of all this? Parliament has been striving to make the working classes fitter and fitter for the franchise . . .

W.E. Gladstone, from a speech to the House of Commons, 12 April 1866.

Eventually, in 1867, a Second Reform Act was passed giving the vote in the boroughs to male householders and lodgers paying £10 a year. In the counties £12 householders were given the vote. With this, the number of voters almost doubled to just under 2 million. The act also took account of the migration of population by taking 45 seats from boroughs with less than 10,000 people and redistributing them. Twenty-five were given to the counties and the rest to large towns.

In 1872 secret ballot was introduced to the delight of people such as the anonymous writer of this letter printed in a contemporary newspaper.

F Sir,
With the ballot, farmers will be better able to return a different set of men to the House of Commons. Hitherto farmers have been compelled to vote for a nominee of the landlords. Hence it is that county members are generally landowners, and their kinsfolk and tools . . .

The landowners stink and swarm in Parliament and are a nuisance to be got rid of. We shall not have honest laws until many landowners are replaced by working men.
A Warwickshire Labourer

A letter to the editor of Reynoldson's Newspaper, 21 July 1872.

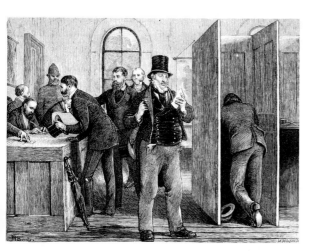

G Methods of voting before and after 1872: the hustings and voting by ballot.

It was 1884 before male household suffrage was extended to the counties, raising the number of voters from 2 to 5 million. Women, male domestic servants and others still did not have the vote. Since 1858 MPs did not need to own land but they still did not receive wages.

?

1 a) According to the Duke of Wellington, (source D), who had power after 1832?

b) Study source A. Explain how this is not true by looking at the following:
   (i) new seats for town and county
   (ii) new voters in town and county
   (iii) method of voting
   (iv) men who were MPs.

2 What were the reasons for the rise of Chartism in the 1830s?

3 Describe the aims of the Chartists and explain how they would help the working class.

4 Why did the Chartist movement fail?

5 How useful is source D for explaining the failure of the Chartist movement?

6 How far had Britain become democratic by the end of the nineteenth century?

*T*HE POWER OF THE UNIONS

• •

● *The Development of Trade Unions*

Low wages and bad conditions in the early nineteenth century made trade unions necessary, but they were illegal until 1824 when the government repealed the Combination Laws. Most unions were local and attached to one industry, but they were not very effective in raising wages or improving conditions. In the early 1830s there were two attempts to form a national union for all workers. The most famous was the Grand National Consolidated Trades Union (GNCTU), formed in 1833 and led by Robert Owen.

H The design of the union is in the first instance to increase wages and to cut down the hours of labour. But the great and final aim of it must be to set up a different order of things which will give the working classes more say in how the things they produce are used.

Robert Owen, 1834.

Within a few months the union had half a million supporters and Owen threatened to call a general strike. The country would come to a stop until the government was forced to grant better conditions.

This did not happen as employers 'blacklisted' union leaders and locked workers out of the factories until they signed 'the document'.

I We, the undersigned . . . do hereby declare that we are not in any way connected with the General Union of . . . and that we do not and will not contribute to the support of such members of the said union as are or may be out of work in consequence of belonging to such union.

Brief History of the Operative Building Trades' Union, 1833.

The government also helped end the GNCTU when, in 1834, it allowed six farm labourers from Tolpuddle in Dorset to be transported to Australia for seven years as punishment for forming a trade union and taking secret oaths. Two years of petitions and marches were needed to win them a pardon and it was 1838 before they returned home.

J This picture from the GNCTU newspaper shows trade unionists at a meeting at Copenhagen Fields, 21 April 1834.

● *Craft Unions*

By 1839 the GNCTU was long dead. Trade Union membership dropped from 800,000 in 1834 to 100,000 in 1842.

With low wages and increased unemployment caused by trade slumps, workers could not afford to pay subscriptions to organisations which did not help them. They turned instead to Chartism, until it too failed them.

It was not until the 1850s that organisations such as the Amalgamated Society of Engineers (ASE) appeared. They were skilled, well-paid workers whose weekly subscription was 1 shilling (5p) and their aim was to keep wages high by limiting the number of their workers.

Stonemasons had this to say about strikes.

K Keep from them as you would from a ferocious animal that you know would destroy you.

The Stonemasons' Central Committee, Fortnightly Circular, December 1845.

These 'craft' unions did well but others were less fortunate.

EFFECTS OF A STRIKE

UPON THE CAPITALIST   AND   UPON THE WORKING MAN.

L 'Effects of the strike on the capitalist and the working man', *Punch* 1852.

● *New Model Unionism*

The unions modelled on the ASE were successful in the 1850s but they only represented a small proportion of workers.

Other workers became frustrated. In 1866 a non-union worker was killed in Sheffield when his house was bombed during a steel strike. The following year a trade union was unable to get back money which had been embezzled from it by it's secretary. After a government enquiry two acts were passed. The 1871 Trade Union Act protected union funds while the Conspiracy and Protection of Property Act 1875 allowed peaceful picketing – to stop 'blacklegs' working.

?

1 According to source H, what were the three aims of the GNCTU?

2 Explain what each of the following did to discourage workers joining the GNCTU:
   a) employers
   b) government.

3 In what ways were the 'craft' unions which appeared in the 1850s different from the GNCTU?

?

1 In what ways did the aims of the GNCTU differ from earlier unions?

2 Why did the GNCTU fail?

3 How useful is source J in explaining why the Tolpuddle Martyrs were given a pardon?

4 Describe the new unions of the 1850s.

5 How far do sources K and L agree about the effects of strikes? Explain your answer.

6 How far had the position of trade unions improved by 1875?

7 POPULAR CULTURE

● *Working-class Leisure and Entertainment 1830-80*

In some ways the title is misleading. For many working-class people there was little time for leisure. Working hours were long; twelve hours a day, six days a week, was common. Even when work was finished, most people were too tired to enjoy themselves.

On summer evenings and Sundays, those who could, went for walks in the nearby country; but as towns grew bigger, and coal mines and iron workings spread over the land, this became more difficult. In the coalfields and large cities drunkenness became more common. In rural areas, much more entertainment had to be provided by the people themselves. In the Highlands, the local people kept alive the celidh traditions. Piping, songs and stories were one way of preserving their way of life. Those forced to emigrate (see p 6) took these traditions with them to Glasgow, Canada and America. In the farming areas of eastern Scotland, there was a similar style of entertainment. In the North East, farm workers lived together in bothies, often little better than sheds. The long winter evenings were spent singing local songs, later known as 'bothy ballads'. (Over a quarter of Scotland's traditional songs come from Aberdeenshire.) By the 1860s and 1870s, wages for skilled craftsmen, at least, in the towns had improved. Some were able to join sports clubs for activities such as curling.

A Melrose Curling Club.

Perhaps the most important change at this time was the introduction of the half day on Saturdays. This gave working people more leisure than ever before. One result was the huge growth of spectator sports, especially football. Many of Scotland's senior clubs were founded in the 20 years after 1870.

B This photograph shows the Rangers' team which played in the Scottish Cup Final in the 1876/7 season, when they lost to Vale of Leven by 3 goals to 2.

1. Why did working people not have many leisure activities before the 1870s? Find at least two reasons.

2. What kinds of leisure activities were common in rural areas such as the Highlands and the North East?

3. What kinds of activities became more popular in the towns after 1860?

4. What two reasons were there for their growth in popularity?

● *Upper and Middle-class Leisure 1830–80*

Better-off people largely made their own entertainment, though in much greater comfort than the working class. The photographs below shows evening entertainments at Bridge of Weir, Renfrewshire and Moniaive, Dumfriesshire around 1880.

C

D

Out of doors, families and clubs of men took part in sports such as croquet or bowls.

E   A family playing croquet.

F   Men playing bowls.

For the very wealthy, there were other outdoor sports. Some people had private yachts, while others preferred the excitement of hunting, shooting and fishing. Rich businessmen from Central Scotland and England bought estates in the Highlands for this purpose. Although this gave some employment, many highlanders resented their new masters; they also resented the way the land was kept tied up from other uses such as farming. The owners had no such qualms; here a group proudly show off their day's 'bag' (see page 38).

G

Finally, there was the game Scotland gave to the world – golf. Groups of industrialists, business- and professional men formed clubs in or near the big cities.

H This photograph shows the members of Glasgow Golf Club at their Annual Competition in Alexandra Park in 1880.

Spectator sports, especially football and rugby, heightened Scots' sense of identity.

I Rivalry with England was the oxygen that kept the fire of Scottish football burning. Here was an area where Scotland could compete against its much bigger and wealthier neighbour . . . the Scots sense of nationhood . . . could assert itself.

Bill Crampsey, *The Scottish Football League: The First 100 Years*

?

1 Describe some of the main indoor pastimes of wealthier people.

2 What were their main outdoor pursuits?

3 In what ways were the leisure pursuits of the wealthier classes different from the working classes?

4 Do you agree that Scottish leisure pursuits at this time were largely Scottish in origin? Give evidence to support your point of view.

SECTION B

1880-1939

8 CHANGING BRITAIN

● *The Economy*

At the end of the nineteenth century Britain controlled an empire covering almost a quarter of the world. From the 1850s her industry and trade were so strong she regarded herself as 'the workshop of the world'. She was able to sell her goods more cheaply than other countries and this meant cheaper goods at home, high profits for businessmen and an improvement in wages for the workers.

People in Britain thought this would continue and few noticed the worrying signs. Britain's main industries were coal, cotton and wool, iron and steel and heavy engineering. Yet by the end of the century the USA was the world's leading producer of coal and by 1908 Germany was producing twice as much steel as Britain.

This situation was made worse by the First World War. Industry was geared to war production and Britain lost many markets for her goods. British industries were slow to invest money in things like oil and electricity and this made it more difficult to compete with other countries.

● *Society*

A

Class	% Population	Jobs	Yearly Income
UPPER	0.5	landowners	£2,000 +
MIDDLE Upper	2.5	bankers, industrialists, judges, doctors	£1-2,000
Lower	17.0	shopkeepers clerks, teachers	£150-500
WORKING Skilled	80.0	engineers, joiners, foremen	£100-150
Unskilled		labourers	£35-55

B The better-off classes lived in comfort: a drawing room in 1895.

British society before the First World War was divided into three classes separated by birth, education, life-style and wealth.

By 1900 almost three-quarters of the people of Britain were living in the towns and cities.

Improvements for the working class were coming very slowly. Compulsory education, trade unions and the First World War led to votes for all, forcing political parties to support more social reform, as the working class made up the biggest number of voters by the 1920s.

?

1 Describe two ways Britain was a rich country before 1900.

2 a) Which countries were able to produce more coal and steel than Britain before 1914?
   b) Why did Britain's trade decline after the First World War?

3 Study source A. Draw a circle. Now colour it in showing the percentage of people in the three main classes.

4 What changes forced governments to pay more attention to the conditions of the working class?

Urbanisation

The population was growing by about 1 per cent per year and by 1900 large towns were expanding so quickly they were swallowing up villages. Between 1871 and 1900 the number of British towns with a population over 100,000 rose from 14 to 33.

C

	1801	1851	1901
London	957,000	2,362,000	4,536,000
Glasgow	77,000	329,000	776,000
Liverpool	82,000	376,000	704,000
Manchester	70,000	303,000	645,000
Birmingham	71,000	233,000	523,000
Sheffield	46,000	135,000	407,000
Cardiff	–	18,000	164,000

Although poverty was still as great among the working class, education, made compulsory in 1870 in England and Wales and 1872 in Scotland, was slowly bringing changes. Working-class newspapers like the *Daily Mail* (1896) and the *News of the World* had a circulation of over a million and gave short articles on crime and sport. Although they simplified issues they were capable of influencing public opinion and the politicians. The Liberal Government of 1906-14 found itself passing reforms to stop working-class voters changing over to the new Labour Party.

Trade Union membership which had been 4 million in 1914 rose to 8.3 million by 1920 and, despite the failure of the 1926 General Strike, the partnership of Trade Unions and the Labour Party helped bring about social reform. The trade depression of the 1930s, with 22 per cent unemployment in 1932, slowed down improvements in the standard of living but there was no doubt that parliament had to be responsible to the whole nation, not just to a privileged minority.

?

1 In what ways was Britain a strong, influential country in the second half of the nineteenth century?

2 To what extent had her position weakened by the end of the 1930s?

3 Draw a pie chart showing the different classes in Britain around 1900.

4 Draw a bar graph comparing the annual incomes of the following people:
landowner, banker, shopkeeper, engineer, labourer.

D 'Back-to-back' houses, like these, were built in many expanding cities at the end of the nineteenth century. They saved space, so there was room for more houses and more people.

9 PEOPLE AT WORK

● *Farming and the First World War*

When war broke out in 1914, the importance of agriculture was soon realised. In that year Britain produced only one-fifth of the wheat she needed. If supplies of food from overseas were cut off, Britain would soon starve.

The biggest problem was getting people to work on the land. Many men had joined the armed forces. Posters like this one appeared in 1915 and after.

A Poster encouraging women to join the Land Army.

As a result many women started work on the land; ploughing, sowing, hoeing, harvesting and driving tractors. Without women like these Britain would have starved.

B Land Army women working in an Essex cornfield.

The government also controlled wages and prices. Food production soon increased. Wheat and potato output rose by 60 per cent. The people of Britain were able to eat better than those in Germany, where they suffered severe food shortages.

When the war ended, agriculture was less important. Both prices and wages fell sharply. People left the land in growing numbers, looking for a better life in the cities, or abroad.

?

1 Why did agriculture become important when war broke out?

2 Why was the work of the Women's Land Army important?

3 What effects did the end of the war have on farming?

CHANGES ON THE LAND

Despite its importance during the First World War, agriculture had entered a long period of decline. Between 1870 and 1914 the number of people employed in agriculture fell by 25 per cent, while the population rose by 40 per cent. Wheat prices fell from 55s per quarter in 1870 to 33s in 1914, and only 7s in 1939. The area growing wheat fell from 3.6 m acres in 1872 to 1.7 m acres in 1914, and stayed at that level in 1939, despite the wartime rise to 2.6 m acres.

The government set up two Royal Commissions to examine the problem, in 1879 and 1893. Their findings were:
- Foreign competition: transport developments, especially steamships and railways, meant that cheap food, mainly wheat and refrigerated meat, flooded into Britain.
- New foods: traditional foods like butter were facing competition from substitutes like margarine.
- Bad weather: six wet summers, between 1873 and 1879, had reduced crops when farmers needed them most. In 1879 alone, sheep rot had caused the death of 3 million sheep.

There was little the government could do, because it did not want to abandon the policy of Free Trade. Also, the bulk of the population was benefiting from cheaper food prices – a 4lb loaf cost 7d (3p) in 1880, 6d (2½p) in 1890 and only ½d (2p) in 1900. Falling food prices meant that people could afford to eat better – meat, milk, butter and vegetable consumption all rose steadily.

Farmers who changed to these products prospered. The area growing fruit doubled between 1873 and 1907. Grassland for animals and poultry increased by 6m acres in the same period, while acres under wheat and barley fell by 2m.

C

Year	Cattle	Sheep	Pigs	Horses
1872	5.6m	27.9m	2.7m	1.2m
1913	6.9m	23.9m	2.2m	1.3m
1939	8.1m	25.9m	2.7m	.9m

P Matthias, The First Industrial Nation.

After the war, agriculture's decline continued. In Scotland, between 1921 and 1938, farm output fell from £48m to £40m. A new reason for this decline was a change in government policy.

Subsidies paid for sugar beet (after 1925) and wheat (after 1932) benefited the south and east of England; only 6 per cent of the subsidies went to Scotland. Many Scottish farmers decided to try their luck in the south.

D News about East Anglia got about fast. A better climate, easier working soil, with no damn great lumps of granite pushing out of it.

Ronald Blythe, Akenfield.

Those who stayed made the best of it. Some tried to introduce new machinery, like this

E A tractor pulling a reaper-binder in 1936.

?

1 Draw a table to show the decline in agriculture in this period. Use data for the years 1870/2, 1914 and 1939.

2 What was the main reason for the decline in British agriculture after the 1870s? Justify your answer.

3 Was all agriculture in trouble at this time? Again, explain your answer.

4 Why did some Scottish farmers move south in the 1930s?

*I*NDUSTRY: GROWTH AND DECLINE

For Scotland's industries, this period tells two very different stories. Until 1914, Scotland had been the home of prosperous heavy industries; after the First World War, these industries were faced with serious difficulties.

● *Textiles*

Cotton textiles were the first industry to use factory methods. They were also the first to feel the problems that other industries would later face.

F	Total Output (Million lbs)	Cloth Exports (Million yds)	Thread Exports (Million lbs)
1880s	1,473	4,675	267
1910s	1,864	5,460	202
1930s	1,360	1,970	152

P Matthias, The First Industrial Nation.

?

1   What two pieces of evidence show that the cotton industry was growing until the end of the First World War in 1918?

2   What two pieces of evidence show that the cotton industry was depressed after 1918?

Writing in 1963, MW Flynn summarised the reasons for the decline of the British cotton industry:

G 1   <u>Failure to adopt new machinery</u> – the automatic loom and electric drive were not adopted as quickly as in other countries.
2   <u>Labour relations</u> – workers were not keen to adopt two or three shift working.
3   <u>Foreign competition</u> – cotton is the first industry many countries turn to when they begin to industrialise; India and Japan, which were major markets for British goods, started their own industries. By the 1930s they were even selling cotton goods to Britain.
4   <u>Competition from new industries</u> – artificial fibres like rayon, nylon, and terylene replaced cotton for many purposes during the second quarter of the twentieth century.

M W Flynn, An Economic and Social History of British since 1700, *1963.*

?

1   Can the problems of the cotton industry be blamed on either management or workers? Explain your answer.

● *Coal*

The coal industry also had mixed fortunes in this period.

H	Total Output (million tons)	Exports (million tons)	Employment (thousands)
1880	156	20	504
1910	270	65	1094
1930	220	43	780

Working conditions remained dangerous. In the years 1922 to 1924, no less than 597,198 miners were injured. Boys as young as 14 were legally allowed to work underground in this most dangerous industry, as this photograph shows.

I A young boy working in the mines.

There were no facilities at the pit head. Miners had to bathe and dry their clothes at home, which was often a three mile walk from the mine.

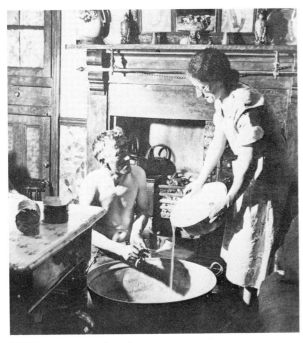

J A miner bathing.

K Clothes drying at the fireside.

1 Compare the table (source H) with the table showing the cotton industry (source F). What similarities can you see?

2 What effect did the decline of the mining industry have on miners after 1910?

3 What evidence is there that working in the mines was
   a) unpleasant
   b) dangerous?

M W Flynn explains the decline of mining after the First World War with the following reasons:

L Labour in the mines remained cheap; there was little incentive for mine owners to equip mines with mechanical cutters.

Electricity began to compete effectively with coal in both the home and factory.

Governments of foreign coal-producing countries began subsidising their exports; Britain lost markets such as Scandinavia.

Mine owners tried to cut wages in order to cut costs; this caused a series of disputes, the most serious being in 1926. Then the miners were on strike for six months.

M W Flynn, An Economic and Social History of Britain since 1700, *1963.*

M The inefficiency of British industries is by no means exclusively due to the workers who have tried to limit output, but also to the manufacturers and to the Government. British employers have been too conservative. They have neglected new processes and inventions, they have relied for success rather on cheap labour than on the utmost efficiency in organisation.

Sir Leo Money MP, 1918.

1 Match the causes of the decline in mining (source L) with the headings underlined in source G.

2 How far does Flynn agree with Sir Leo Money (source M)?

● *Shipbuilding: Old and New*

The shipbuilding industry had grown quickly in this period, mainly because of the huge growth of Britain's trade with overseas countries.

There were several changes in the way ships were built. Around 1880 wooden ships were becoming rare; newer ships were built of iron, and later, steel. Secondly, steamships were replacing sailing ships, because they did not depend on a good wind. Lastly, ships were becoming larger, so they could sail further, and carry more.

N This photograph shows Alexander Hall's shipyard in Aberdeen (c.1880).

0 This photograph was taken at John Brown's shipyard in Clydebank. Work has just resumed on the 'Queen Mary'.

Working in shipyards was dangerous and hard work.

P Shortly before 10 o'clock on Friday morning, John Connolly, a ship-plater, lost his life at Fairfield Shipbuilding Yard. While climbing a ladder into the boilerhold he overbalanced and fell 32 feet. Two other accidents also occurred in the Fairfield Yards. Charles Scott, 17, a template boy, fell from the top of a ladder – 30 feet – and suffered serious injuries to his neck and back; and John Miller, a plater, lost two of the fingers of his left hand by a steel plate falling on them.

The Govan Press, *24 August 1900.*

A major complaint of the men was their lack of job security. They could be laid off at only two hours' notice. They tried to combat this by jealously guarding their own craft. For example, joiners worked on wood less than 1½ ins thick, and carpenters did the work if it was over that thickness. These rules agreed between crafts were called demarcation. Management often called them 'restrictive practices'.

?

1   Why did the shipbuilding industry grow quickly at this time?

2   In what three ways did the building of ships change?

3   What differences are there between the two shipyards?

4   What dangers did men working in shipyards face?

5   What other complaints about working conditions were held by
a) workers
b) management?

Good Times, Bad Times for Shipbuilding

Scotland benefited more than most areas from the growth of shipbuilding. It had cheap steel, skilled workers and deep sheltered rivers for launching. This was one reason that Yarrows moved from London to the Clyde in 1906. Many Scottish firms gained from the big expansion of the Royal Navy between 1906 and 1914. By this time one fifth of the world's ships were built in Scotland. The Clyde, in particular, was lined with shipyards from Glasgow to Dumbarton, and with more at Greenock and Port Glasgow.

When the First World War ended the prosperity continued. Shipowners in this country rushed to replace ships that had been sunk in the war. But by 1921 the stream of orders dried up. The 1920s were hard. Many shipyard workers were laid off.

In 1929 a panic on the American stock market led to the selling of millions of shares. This was called the Wall Street Crash and it led to a world trade depression. No-one needed new ships. Shipyards closed down all over the country. Probably the worst-hit town was Jarrow, near Newcastle; it depended on Palmer's Shipyard, the town's only industry. The yard got no orders at all in 1932. To help the industry out of its difficulties, a group of yard owners formed a company called the National Shipbuilding Security Ltd. It bought up yards in order to share out the few orders going. In 1934 it bought Palmer's and closed it down. A Special Correspondent of *The Times* wrote, on 21 March 1934:

Q One feels, sometimes strongly and angrily, that London still has no idea of the troubles that face the industrial north. In London and the South, for every 84 men working, there are 14 out of work. In Jarrow, a formerly prosperous town of 32,000 inhabitants, for every 25 working, there are 75 out.

Scotland suffered almost as badly. Groups of unemployed men hung about street corners, as shown in this photograph.

R

In 1939, the Scottish Economic Committee summed up the situation:

S Shipbuilding occupies a key position, both in itself, and through the dependence on it of the steel industry and others down to the furniture needed for passenger vessels. Any contraction in world trade has a depressing effect not only on shipbuilding, but on a whole group of industries. A further difficulty arises owing to subsidised competition from foreign shipbuilding industries. Rising costs, partly due to rearmament, threatens to end any orders for merchant shipping.

The Scottish Economic Committee, 1939.

Government help ensured that the 'Queen Mary' was completed by John Brown's of Clydebank.

?

1 What evidence is there that shipbuilding was an important industry in this period?

2 Explain fully why shipbuilding was in difficulties after 1921.

3 What effects did the difficulties faced by shipbuilding have on the towns that depended on it?

4 Was the Special Correspondent of *The Times* sympathetic to the problems of such areas? Explain your answer.

5 In your opinion, did the government do enough to help shipbuilding between 1919 and 1939? Give reasons for your answer.

NEW INDUSTRIES

Before 1914 Britain had depended on older industries like cotton, coal and shipbuilding. Most of Britain's older industries were in the north of the country. These were the ones worst hit by the depression in trade after 1929. The south of the country was much less affected. The main reason for this was the growth there of new industries like car manufacturing and electrical goods production.

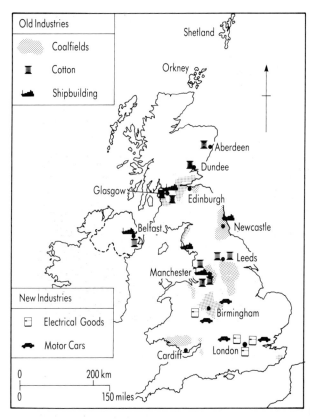

T Old and new industries in Britain.

Work in these new industries was much more pleasant than in older industries. For a start, work was usually indoors; factories were smaller, cleaner and brighter; they were much less dangerous, and often the wages were better. As these industries were growing, there was much less chance of being unemployed.

U This photograph shows work on the assembly line of the Morris Company at Cowley, outside Oxford.

Mass production methods were common in these new industries, but not everyone liked them. Walter Greenwood, writing in 1939, said:

V Any man of spirit preferred the dole to the high pay that could be earned. I was not used to mixing with men who put up with such regimentation. I found them spineless, money-grabbing and selfish. They didn't care about other workers.

Walter Greenwood, How the Other Man Lives, 1939.

?

1   Which new industries grew after 1919?

2   In what five ways were conditions better for workers in these industries than in the old industries?

3   Do you agree that the car industry is a mass production industry? Explain your answer.

4   What three words show that Greenwood did not like the type of man that worked in the car industry? (Source V.)

● The Growth of the Electrical Industry

One result of the depression after 1929 was that the price of many goods fell. This meant that those people in work could actually buy more – or save. Many people took the opportunity to buy a house, encouraged by the government's policy of low interest rates. Millions of houses were built in the 1930s, especially in the more prosperous south.

W Edgware, near London, in 1923.

X Edgware in 1948.

To live in these new homes, people needed electrical power, domestic gadgets such as vacuum cleaners, and, to get about, a car. Because the largest market for these goods was in the south, most of the new industries were located there. The growing demand for electricity led to the government setting up the National Grid in 1926. This enabled power generated in one part of the country to be used in another. The British Association said of the Grid:

> **Y** The biggest single factor in bringing us out of the slump has been the National Grid. Construction started in 1927, and was complete in 1933. At the end of 1937 the Grid had 4,180 miles of transmission lines, linking up generating stations with a capacity of 7½ million kilowatts.
>
> The total cost was about £27,800,000. Most of the building was done in the slump years, 1930-1933. The Board was able to take advantage of falling prices, so cutting the cost.

The British Association, Britain in Recovery, *1938.*

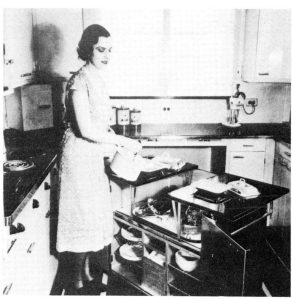

Z Many of the new houses built in the 1930s featured kitchens full of electric gadgets.

?

1 In what ways did the Depression actually help the growth of the new industries?

2 Why did the boom in housebuilding lead to growth in other industries?

3 To what extent did government policies help the growth of these industries? Give reasons for your answers.

RAILWAYS AT THEIR PEAK
1880-1914

• •

In 1914, Britain's railways were at their peak. The London & North Western Railway was the largest joint stock company in the world. Most railway companies had earned large profits for years. Some of these profits had been passed on to the shareholders, the rest had been put back into the business.

Bigger locomotives made journeys faster; better carriages made journeys more comfortable; better stations made arrival more pleasant. The changes can be seen by comparing two trains. The trains in source AA ran on the Liverpool & Manchester in the 1830s; the other (source BB) of London & North Western coaches, is pulled by a Caledonian Railway locomotive, built in 1903. It was the most powerful in Britain at that time.

AA

BB 'Cardean' (No.903) waits in Central Station, Glasgow, with the London train, around 1910.

CC This picture shows Wemyss Bay station, on the Firth of Clyde, where company steamers waited for commuters and day trippers.

The companies also advertised their facilities widely.

DD Central Station, Glasgow.

They built hotels like Turnberry, Cruden Bay and Gleneagles.

EE Gleneagles Hotel, built in 1923.

The railway network in Britain reached its greatest extent at this time. The Firth of Forth was bridged in 1890, while lines were also driven into the highlands.

FF The Forth Bridge being built in the late 1880s.

?

1 Compare the trains from the 1830s (source AA) with the one from the early twentieth century (source BB). What improvements can you see?

2 How did railway companies try to attract more passengers? (Try to find at least four ways.)

● *The Railways in Difficulties*

Only 20 years after the railways had reached their peak, they were almost bankrupt. There were three major reasons for this.

- During the First World War the government took over the railways. The railway companies were busier than ever, but repairs to trains and tracks were not made as often as they should have been. This happened because workshops had to concentrate on making guns and munitions. When the war ended many railways were in a poor state.

- War had also encouraged the development of more efficient ways of manufacturing lorries and cars. For the first time railways faced serious competition from another form of transport.

- In the years after 1919 many industries found themselves in difficulties as trade and demand for their goods declined. This included heavy industry such as steel-making and mining – two of the railways' best customers!

The railways did try to attract customers by running new, faster trains such as the Royal Scot and the Flying Scotsman.

To help the railways become more competitive, in 1923 the government grouped them into four large companies, the Southern, Great Western, London Midland Scottish and London and North Eastern Railways.

?

1 Summarise the reasons for the railways' problems after 1919.

2 How helpful was the government towards the railways, in your opinion? Again, justify your answer.

Group Activity
Form small groups; each is to be the Board of Directors of one of the new companies. What plans would you put forward to make your company profitable? Remember that the government will not give you any money to invest, and banks are not likely to lend you any. (Any group that comes up with more than two ideas deserves a prize!)

*T*HE MOTOR CAR ARRIVES

The motor car was developed in the 1880s, but its high cost made it the plaything of the rich. Car owners went for leisurely drives, and were sometimes competitors in rallies.

GG This photograph was taken on the 'Rest and be Thankful' road in Argyll in 1907.

The mass-production of motor vehicles during and after the First World War led to a greater availability of cheaper vehicles, and more people took to the roads.

HH This photograph was taken in Tooting, a London Suburb, in 1922.

Other types of motor vehicles appeared, as shown by this photograph taken in Edinburgh.

II A baker's delivery van.

The spread of car ownership into the middle classes meant changes in house layout.

KK These traffic lights in London were one of the first sets in use in 1926.

The government had to introduce measures to control the problems caused by traffic. They also had to make the roads safer. The first traffic lights appeared in London in 1926. In 1934 the pedestrian crossing (the 'Belisha Beacon') was introduced. The 30mph speed limit was abolished in 1930, but when road deaths reached 7,000 per year, it was brought back in built-up areas.

JJ The space outside this house allows room for a garage and a separate garden gate.

?

1 Why did only rich people have motor cars before the First World War?

2 Why did cars become more common after 1918?

3 What problems arose as more people owned cars?

● *Transport in Town*

Perhaps the biggest change in this period was the development of transport in urban areas. One of the biggest changes, the growth of motor transport, has already been mentioned. Richard Tames gives the reason for this growth:

LL The petrol-driven vehicle offered many advantages. It could go almost anywhere. The manufactuer and the shopkeeper with deliveries to make saw obvious advantages in door-to-door service and freedom from the railway timetable. Motor transport was faster over short distances and in towns. It was often cheaper as road haulage companies were free to pick their customers and offer special rates, while the railways were required to charge the same to all users and to run trains in country areas, whether they made a profit or not.

Richard Tames, Railways, 1970.

New vehicles appeared in ever greater numbers during the 1920s and 30s. Bus services also developed, like the one in Aberdeen.

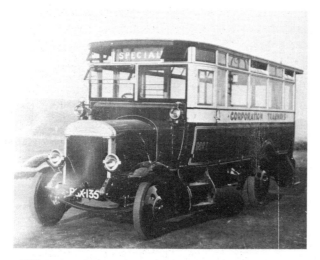

MM Aberdeen's first motor bus.

The other major change in town transport was the development of the tramcar. The earliest ones were often run by private firms.

Tramcars had several advantages in towns. They were able to run an intensive service, with only a few minutes between cars, right through

NN A tramcar belonging to the Edinburgh Northern Tramway Company, which was started in 1896.

city centre streets, where they made frequent stops. Large numbers of people could be moved quickly, and they were cheap! The journey from Paisley to Airdrie, a distance of 20 miles, cost the princely sum, in 1919, of 1p.

?

1   According to Tames, what advantages did motor vehicles have? (Source LL.)

2   What advantages did tramcars have in towns?

Activity
Your group is the Council Transport Committee of a town around 1900. You have been asked to decide which form of transport the town should adopt:
tramcars; motor buses; or suburban railways.
Think about the following factors:
● cost of building
● cost of buying vehicles
● cost of operating
● convenience to the public
● the amount of control you will have.
   Then prepare a report for the Council saying which form of transport you are recommending, with your reasons, and why you have rejected the others.

WOMEN AND WORK

At the beginning of this century, domestic service was the most common job for women. One author describes their work:

OO There were no labour-saving devices, and they usually worked a grinding day of about fourteen hours. Many were housed in cold cramped attics, fed on left-overs, and allowed only half a day free a fortnight.

Women's Rights, 1971.

Even worse off were those who worked as seamstresses, making clothes. They were paid 1p an hour and had to pay for their own needles, thread and candles! Many people at the time called this a 'sweated trade'; to earn enough to live, they had to work 16 hours a day, every day. Women also worked in heavier jobs, such as brick-making and chain-making.

PP These women were employed in brick-making.

Perhaps worst off of all were the match-girls. John Simkin describes the conditions Annie Besant found at Bryant & May's factory in London:

QQ Wages were as low as 20p per week. However they did not always receive their full wages because of a system of fines, ranging from 2p to 5p. Offences included dropping matches and answering back. Besant also discovered that the health of the women had been severely affected by the phosphorus that they used to make the matches.

John Simkin, Trade Unions 1800-1918

Even doing the same jobs as men, the half million women working in Britain's industries earned less than half the pay of men. It was only at the beginning of this century that women were allowed into professions such as medicine and teaching. But even then women teachers who married had to give up their jobs.

?

1   Read source OO. In what ways was life as a domestic servant hard?

2   The description 'sweated trade' means that workers had to work very hard to earn a living. What evidence is there that seamstresses were a sweated trade?

3   What complaints did women match workers at Bryant and May have about
    a) their wages
    b) factory discipline
    c) dangers to health?

4   Many women at this time claimed they were treated unfairly at work. Find as much evidence as you can to support this view.

● *Improvements for Women*

By 1939 the position of women had partly improved. There were several reasons for this:

1   The growth of education; the Acts of 1902 and 1918 extended opportunities for education. They also created a need for more teachers. In Scotland in 1914, 65 per cent of teachers were women – but male teachers were paid almost twice as much.

2   Changes in industry and employment; the growth of light industries such as electrical goods, and service industries, such as banking, made more opportunuties for women. There they could compete on more equal terms.

3   The struggle for votes for women; one reason that some women supported this was that they thought it would lead to more equality in employment. Women over the age of 30 were given the vote in 1918, this was extended to women between 21 and 30 in 1928.

4   The work of trade unions; in 1888 the match-girls of Bryant & May had formed a union and successfully gone on strike for better conditions. Their example encouraged other unskilled workers to form unions. Trade unions tried to increase their membership of women to struggle for better conditions.

5   The effects of the First World War; attitudes to women changed because of the great part played by women, both at home and abroad. Some, like nurses, shared the horrors of the battle-field:

RR   The shells began to scream over-head. In the hospital we found the wounded all yelling like mad things, thinking they were going to be left behind. We sat in the cellars with seventy wounded men to take care of. There was only one line of bricks between us and the shells.

The government was in no doubt about the importance of women to the war effort, as the 1916 poster opposite shows.

SS   A poster encouraging women to enrol as munitions workers.

The overall picture, however, was far from rosy. R Strachey wrote in 1928:

TT   Thousands upon thousands of women workers were dismissed and found no work to do. It is terribly hard on the women. Everyone assumed that they would quietly go back to their homes, but this was impossible. The war had enormously increased the number of surplus women, so that one woman in three had to be self-supporting. Prices were nearly double what they had been in 1914, and the women who had been able to live on their small allowances or fixed incomes could do so no more. The tone of the Press changed. The very same people who had been heroines and saviours of their country a few months before were now parasites, blacklegs and limpets.

R Strachey, The Cause, 1928.

❓

1   Read source TT. Was Strachey sympathetic to the position of women workers after the war? Give evidence to support your answer.

2   Was the war the main reason that the position of women changed in the first 40 years of this century?

10 HOME AND HEALTH

● *Housing*

By 1900 the home life of the upper classes was becoming very comfortable.

A We modernised it with electric light and a telephone. The house contained a large basement, three sitting rooms, a lounge-hall, and seven bedrooms. All the rooms were warmed by coal fires.

We had a staff consisting of a Norland nurse (nanny), a parlourmaid, a housemaid and a cook. The cook earned £28, the nurse £40. We spent about 12 shillings (60p) each week on food and cleaning materials. We bought coal at 15 shillings (75p) a ton.

Mrs C S Peel, Life's Enchanted Cup, *1933.*

The life of the poor was not so pleasant. A Royal Commission on Housing 1884-5 discovered that drains, water supply, building and sanitation were just as bad in many places as they had been in the 1830s. Charles Booth reported this about 1 Tarleton Street, London in 1900.

B The ground floor rooms are occupied by Fletcher, a pedlar, his wife and 6 children. He goes round with a barrow, she does washing and charing. On the first floor in front are Lawson, his wife and 2 children. In the back room lives Bewley with wife and 4 children. They also have a niece of 18 living with them.

Eight feet square – that is about the average of many of these rooms. Walls and ceilings are black with filth. Sewage is running down the walls.

Charles Booth, Life and Labour of the London Poor, *1900.*

Housing Acts from 1890 onwards encouraged local authorities to get rid of the worst of the slums and to build cheap housing. One of the first large-scale housing schemes was in Glasgow, where, in 1906, tenement buildings were planned.

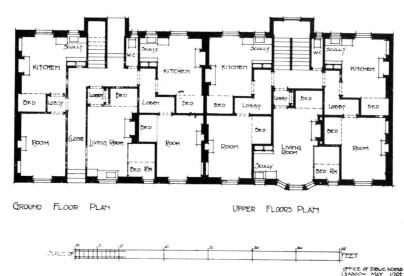

C Kennyhill Tenements, Glasgow, 1906.

It was not until after 1918 that council house building schemes began all over the country. Many of the homes were semi-detached. They cost around £500 to build and the weekly rent of these in York was around 15 shillings 11d (79p) in 1935.

D These council houses in York are typical of the semi-detached houses built after the First World War.

● *Health*

Poor housing was harming the health of the British people. In 1903 recruitment figures for the army showed that 34.6 per cent of all recruits had to be turned away because they were in poor health.

E . . . In our country parish of 2,000, since January 1st 1906, we had had 27 burials, 12 of which have been children aged two and under. Of the last seven, six have been children under 8 months and there are more likely to die. There is no epidemic . . . The doctors know most of the children are poorly fed . . .

A letter from a Surrey clergyman, printed in The Times, 5 October 1906.

Reports like these led the Liberal Government of 1906-14 to introduce medical inspections for school children in 1907 and free treatment for needy children from 1912. The National Health

Insurance Act of 1911 was extended so that it covered 20 million people by 1938.

Many poor people still could not afford to pay for medical care and had to rely on free treatment in the poor law hospitals. The depression of the 1930s made things worse. A survey of 1936 showed that only 30 per cent of the nation was fed properly and that 10 per cent – 4,500,000 people – were very badly fed. This was worst in areas of high unemployment.

?

1   Give five pieces of evidence from source A to show that this family were well-off.

2   a) Draw a box 16 cms square and divide it into quarters.
    b) Label the boxes: upstairs, downstairs, front and back.
    c) In each room write the name of the correct family from 1 Tarleton Street.
    d) In each room put a matchstick figure for each person. Make a child half the size of an adult.

3   Look at source C. Would you prefer to live at Kennyhill or Tarleton Street? Give at least two reasons for your answer.

4   Study source D. In what ways were these council houses better than tenements?

5   What were the real causes of ill-health in Britain at this time?

6   What did the government do to help children and adults?

Group Work
Measure out the size of the rooms in Tarleton Street. Pupils are to play the roles of the people living there. Each family in turn will move into their house. Discuss three problems the family will find.

SUBURBS AND SLUMS

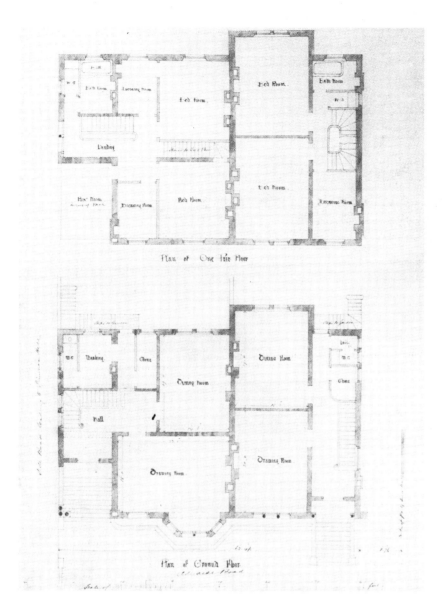

F A Victorian villa.

At the end of the nineteenth century suburbs for the middle classes grew up in most towns. The business and professional man travelled easily and cheaply to work by train, while his family lived well away from the dirt and overcrowding of the town centres. Many of their detached or semi-detached villas can still be seen.

In 1912 the Board of Trade looked into rents being paid by working-class families and wrote this as part of its report about housing in Glasgow.

G The typical house of a working class family is a flat of two or three rooms in a stone-built tenement block, two, three or four stories high. The building is entered by a passage or 'close' leading to a stone stair which goes to the upper floors. Two, three or four flats are found on each floor, and the door by which each flat is entered is on the landing or 'stairhead'. All the rooms in the flat open on to a fair-sized lobby . . . The rooms are large and often had a bed-recess with space for a double bed . . . Some of the family have to sleep in the bed-recess in the living room where the air is more or less polluted. The small number of rooms makes it difficult to separate the sexes in a growing family, or sick children from those who are well and younger children are often disturbed when the older ones go to bed.

Usually each block of flats had a common wash-house and drying ground which the families take turns to use. The most obvious disadvantages . . . are shared toilets and the fact most flats are at the head of one or more flights of stairs.

On the other hand, the tenement has several distinct advantages. It is, as a rule, exceptionally well-built with large high rooms and the workman can live near his work and avoid travelling expenses.

Board of Trade Enquiry into Working-class Rents, 1912.

Between 1919 and 1939 governments had three main aims in housing: to get rid of slums; to build more and better houses and to see that working people paid rents they could afford. However, actual building was slow until the Addison Act of 1919 gave local authorities government subsidies to build around 210,000 houses before grants were cut. Chamberlain's Act of 1923 gave grants to private builders who built 440,000 houses by 1929. Unfortunately, these were too expensive for the people who really needed them. The Wheatley Act of 1924 gave grants to local councils who built 500,000 houses by 1933. However, this did not solve the problems of slums and although Greenwood's Act of 1930 gave council grants to clear slums and rehouse tenants, so resulting in 250,000 slum houses being cleared by 1939, the truth was that more than half a million slum houses still remained.

*H*EALTH AND HOUSING

Government investigations proved the relationship between overcrowding and ill-health. In 1871 32.5 per cent of all Scottish houses had only one room, 37.6 per cent had only two rooms. By 1911 only 12.8 per cent were single rooms and 40.4 per cent were two-roomed houses. The census also showed that in 1911 56 per cent of the single rooms had more than two people living in them. Medical officers

of health reported that in houses of one room 32 per cent of children died before reaching the age of five but that the rate dropped to 2 per cent in houses of five or more rooms.

H Infant Mortality Rate (deaths under 1 year) per 1,000 births.

Year	Glasgow	Scotland
1871	191	130
1881	144	113
1891	148	128
1901	149	129
1911	139	113
1921	106	90
1931	105	82
1941	111	83

Government concern about these figures led to the opening of more than 3,500 welfare clinics for infants and nearly 1,800 ante-natal clinics between 1918 and 1938.

?

1   Study source A.
In what ways were such houses comfortable to live in?

2   Use sources C and G. Make up a table listing the advantages and disadvantages of living in a tenement.

3   What are the main improvements for the working class in the semi-detached houses built after 1921?

4   How far did governments between the wars succeed in their three aims for housing?

5   Use any of the sources to explain what were the real causes of ill-health in Britain in the period 1880-1939.

6   Account for the decline in infant mortality over this period.

Fieldwork
Study your local area and identify as many of the types of housing as you can. If you have a street map of your town you could colour code the different types.

STANDARD OF LIVING AND POVERTY

● *Living in Comfort*

As Britain moved into the twentieth century life improved for a large number of people. The middle and upper classes lived in houses made more comfortable by electricity and machines such as the refrigerator and vacuum cleaner. They ate well and had money for leisure activities such as the music hall and cinema. Some could even afford to buy one of the new motor cars.

A Meals eaten by a rich family of two parents and two children in 1901.
Breakfast: porridge, beefsteak, toast, bread, butter, hot milk, tea
Dinner: minced beef, potatoes, cauliflower, rhubarb pie, cream, oranges
Tea: bread, butter, buns, tarts, pastry, tea
Supper: bread, butter, sweet-cake, cocoa

B S Rowntree, Poverty: a Study of Town Life, 1901.

In the years after the First World War skilled working-class men found themselves earning enough money to improve their lives. A skilled factory workers, earning 75 shillings (£3.75) in 1936, gave his wife 50 shillings (£2.50) for housekeeping. Their family of four spent 1s 6d (8p) on hobbies, the same on tobacco, put 2 shillings (10p) away for a holiday and had 30 shillings (£1.50) a week for food. On Thursday they had:

B Breakfast: boiled eggs, bread, butter, cocoa, cornflakes, milk
Dinner: sausages, potatoes, cabbage, rice pudding
Tea: tea, bread and butter, cooked meat, jam, cakes
Supper: Bread and cheese, milk

B S Rowntree, Poverty and Progress, 1936.

Local council assisted wiring schemes allowed workers to put in electricity and pay back the cost to the council in weekly instalments. From then it was a short step to having a radio or buying other electrical goods.

C A 1930s living room.

D An advertising poster for 'Tarzan'.

Perhaps the greatest change was the fact that many working-class people now had both time and money for leisure pursuits. The cinema was very popular and 990 million tickets were sold in 1938.

Many people who worked inside all week liked to get out into the fresh air; on Saturday afternoons they went to watch their local football teams.

People also liked to bet. Many families filled in their football coupons every week in the hope of winning the big prize which had risen to £25,000 by 1939. Working-class men also liked to risk a few pence on the horses or greyhounds while many pubs ran 'housey-housey' – the 1930s version of bingo. Young, unmarried people liked to go to the 'palais de dance' or dance halls several times each week.

?

1 In what three ways did the lives of the skilled working class improve in the 1920s-30s?

2 a) Draw a table showing the spending of the skilled worker's family in 1936.
   b) What will the remaining 15 shillings (75p) be spent on?

3 List the different ways people could spend their free time in the 1930s. Make one column for men and one for women.

4 Find out about other films made in the 1930s. Design a cinema poster for one of them.

Group Work
a) You are going to interview an older person about 'leisure in the 1930s'. As a group, think of eight good questions to ask.
b) Tape an interview.

E Greyhound racing was very popular. This picture shows the start of a race at White City Stadium, London: one of 187 tracks by 1932.

*I*MPROVED LEISURE

In the 1920s 1.5 million workers had one week's paid holiday per year. In 1938 the Holidays with Pay Act was passed, giving 11 million workers a week's paid holiday. Despite the depression of the 1930s there were greater leisure opportunities for those in work. The British Broadcasting Corporation began in 1926 and by 1932 4.3 million licences had been bought (with possibly as many radio sets without a licence).

In 1928 the first 'talkie' was made in America. In Britain the number of cinemas jumped from 3,000 in 1930 to 4,967 in 1938. Most seats were less than 7d (3p), with some as cheap as 2d (1p) – it is no wonder nearly 20 million cinema tickets were sold each week.

Life was also easier for those who wanted to travel as this account tells us.

F In 1933 there were just over 1,200,000 private cars in use. There were also more than half a million motor cycles . . . 46,000 omnibuses and motor coaches. The average rate of increase was, taking all classes of vehicles, in the terms of about 20 per cent annually. So we find that the motor vehicle from being merely one which ministered to the pleasures of the 'idle rich' has become a vital link in the life of the nation.

Sir Malcolm Campbell, The Roads and the Problem of their Safety, *1937.*

G Billy Butlin opened the first large-scale holiday camp in Skegness in 1937.

The changes in transport also encouraged people to go to holiday resorts like Blackpool and Morecambe in England or Ayr and Rothesay on the Scottish Clyde Coast. The more energetic took up hiking or cycling and by 1938 the Youth Hostel Association had 83,000 members visiting its 300 hostels. It was also at this time the first holiday camps were opened for family holidays.

?

1   Use sources A, B and C. In what three ways were the skilled working class of the 1920s-30s as well off as the middle class before 1914?

2   How would you account for the popularity of the cinema in the 1930s?

3   Make up a table of leisure activities and divide it according to age and sex.

4   How important was improved transport for the boom in leisure?

Research exercise
Research and write up a report on: *either* an interview with an older person about leisure in the 1930s; or plan and work out the cost of a holiday in the 1930s for people from your area. (Local newspapers of the period will be useful for this.)

MAKING ENDS MEET

Although skilled workers could earn anything from 30-40 shillings around 1900, there were others who were very poor. They earned £1 a week or less. The main causes of their poverty were old age, sickness, low wages and unemployment. Despair often led to drunkenness or gambling which made their poverty worse.

B S Rowntree found this was a typical menu for the poor in York around 1900.

H

Day	Breakfast	Lunch/ Dinner	Tea	Supper
Sat	bread butter boiled egg coffee	meat potatoes (fruit) pie tea	tea, bread butter	tea, roast potatoes
Mon	bread butter coffee	meat potatoes bread, tea	tea, bread butter	
Fri	tea, bread butter	tea, bread butter	tea, toast butter	

B S Rowntree, Poverty: a Study of Town Life, 1901.

I Emmeline Pankhurst.

J This is the weekly budget of an ironworker's family from Middlesbrough. The father earned between 18s 6d-23s 9d (92.5p-£1.18) to feed himself, his wife and child.

Item	Cost s d	Cost p
food	7s 5d	37p
rent	5s 6d	27.5p
coal	2s 4d	11.5p
clothing	1s	5p
tobacco	9d	4p
debt	3d	1p
insurance	7d	3p
matches	1d	.5p
lamp oil	2d	1p
1 lb soap	3d	1p
1 packet soap powder	1d	.5p
1 box of polish	1d	.5p
	18s 6d	92.5p

Lady Bell, At the works: a study of a manufacturing town, 1907.

There were many families who could not support themselves and had to go into the workhouse. Emmeline Pankhurst was a poor law guardian in Manchester in 1894 and described workhouse conditions.

K Bread made so much of the ration that hardly anyone ate all of his . . . I was horrified to see girls of 7 and 8 years on their knees scrubbing the cold stones. They were dressed, summer and winter, in thin cotton frocks . . . At night they wore nothing at all . . . I found pregnant women scrubbing floors, until their babies came . . . Old women, over 60 and 70 years, did most of the work, keeping the house clean, sewing . . . a great many were domestic servants . . . who had never earned enough to save or widows whose husbands' pensions had died with them.

My own story, The Autobiography of Emmeline Pankhurst, 1914.

Studies by Rowntree and others showed how much poverty there was, so it is not surprising that the Liberal Government of 1906-14 passed certain reforms: free school meals, old age pensions, health and unemployment insurance.

By 1920 the National Insurance Act was extended to help 12 million workers if they were out of work. From 1929 the local authorities took over the poor law guardians. By 1932 there were 2.7 million unemployed and the insurance fund had a debt of £115 million. In 1934 the Unemployment Insurance Act set up Unemployment Insurance Committees so people could get benefit for the first 15 weeks they were unemployed. After that people had to go to the Unemployment Assistance Board (UAB). There was no right to help from the government. People had to pass the 'means test' to prove they needed money. This caused many problems.

L Since 1919, I earned the standard wage of around £3 a week. My wife and I had been happily married since 1909 and were devoted to each other and our son.

In 1929 my firm went bust and I lost my job . . . By 1931 I was pretty desperate . . . My wife got a job as a house-to-house saleswoman and was able to earn a few shillings a week to add to our dole . . . life became more and more strained . . .

The final blow came when the Means Test was put into operation. They sent me the Means Test form. I knew that a true statement of our family income would stop my benefit. So I was afraid to send it in. When I sent it in they cut my benefit. Both my wife and son, who had just started to earn a few shillings, told me to get out, as I was living on them and the food they needed.

Quoted in RS Lambert and HL Beales, Memoirs of the Unemployed, *1937.*

M The effects of unemployment.

?

1 Give three things which are wrong with the diet of the people in York in 1900.

2 Draw a circle. Mark and colour in the different parts of the Middlesbrough family budget. Every 7.5p will take about 1/12 of the circle (1 hour on a clock face) i.e. food (37p) will take from the top to almost 5 o'clock.

3 What is the only luxury they have?

4 a) What was the workhouse?
   b) Give three types of people who ended up there.

5 **Research exercise**
Find out and write a brief note about the reforms of the 1906-14 Liberal Government mentioned in the text.

6 What was the 'means test'? Why do you think it was unfair? Give at least two reasons for your answer. (Source L.)

SENSIBLE SPENDING

• •

A Dundee newspaper published this account of a working-class family's diet.

N

Breakfast	Porridge and milk, bread and butter, with tea or milk to drink
Dinner	Broth made from a half pound of boiling beef, with a penny (d) worth of leek, carrots, turnip and a half penny worth barley. Sometimes the boiled meat was served with potatoes as a second course. Occasionally there was a pudding, usually rice.
Tea	Bread and butter spread with jam or syrup and tea to drink, but a working father might also have fish, meat or cold meat as an extra.
Supper	There was no regular supper but hungry children might be given a piece of bread and butter at bedtime.

Dundee Social Union Study, 1905.

Source O is a list of prices from 1907.

O

Item	Cost	Qty
Foodstuffs		
Apples (dried)	6d	lb
bacon	4.5	lb
bacon end (soup)	5.5	lb
beef or mutton	9	lb
biscuits	4d	lb
breakfast flakes	3d	lb
bread	3d	2 lb
butter	14d	lb
cheese	12d	lb
chicken	18d	each
coffee	12.5	lb
corned beef (tin)	10.5	2 lb
dripping (lard)	5d	lb
eggs	18d	doz
flour	9d	7 lb
jam strawberry	6d	lb
liver	4d	lb
milk	.5d	pint
oatmeal	1.5d	lb
onions	1d	lb
peaches	18d	tin
pears	15d	tin
potatoes	.5d	lb
rice	4d	lb
sugar	4.5	2lb
tea	13d	lb

Luxuries

chocolate caramels	6d	4 oz
mild beer	1.5d	pint
whisky	2d	nip
whisky	36d	bot
Wills Capstan cigarettes	12d	pkt 50

The Army and Navy Stores Catalogue, 1907.

Life for the unemployed in the 1930s was also very difficult. In 1936 a husband, wife and four children had about 36 shillings a week to live on. Rowntree in his study *Poverty and Progress* recorded their spending as follows:

P

Rent	7 shillings
Clothing	2s 3d
food	16s 10d
husband	2s
light and fuel	3s 6d
household sundries (soap etc)	1s 10d
burial insurance	2s 6d

B S Rowntree, Poverty and Progress, 1936.

?

1. Study sources H and N. Which was the healthier diet? Give three reasons for your answer.

2. **Group exercise**
   Make up a healthy menu for the family in source J and draw up a shopping list with costs, using the prices in source O.

3. a) What was wrong with workhouse conditions in the 1890s (source I)? Give at least four faults.
   b) What do you think were the aims of the poor law guardians?

4. **Research exercise**
   Find out and write paragraphs on the main social reforms of the Liberal Government 1906-14.

5. Do you think the 'means test' was fair? Justify your answer.

6. Study sources J and P.
   Draw 2 pie charts comparing the spending of poor families 1900 and 1930s.
   Divide spending into the following categories: rent, food, clothing, fuel, insurance, sundries, luxuries.

POWER TO THE PEOPLE

● *The Vote . . . For Men*

The Reform Act of 1867 had given the vote to male householders in the boroughs who paid the poor rate, and lodgers paying £10 a year rent. In the counties a householder had to pay £12 a year rent before he could vote. The Ballot Act of 1872 allowed the new voters to vote in secret. The people of the counties wanted the same rights as those in the boroughs.

A Bill to extend the vote in the counties was introduced in 1884. The House of Lords tried to delay it but working-class newspapers protested.

> **A** We are not asking to alter the representation of the Lords, much as it needs alteration . . . The Commons, that is the people who are not lords – wish to be more fully represented, especially those people who are not represented at this time . . . If the people are agreed, there is an end of the matter.
>
> Reynold's Newspaper, *6 July 1884*.

When the 1884 Reform Act was passed it gave male householders the vote in both boroughs and counties. Although there were now around 5,000,000 electors, no women were allowed to vote, nor were men servants who worked in rich people's houses.

Many people felt the House of Lords, which was not elected, had too much power to stop the passing of new laws agreed to by the elected MPs in the House of Commons.

Greater education opportunities for the working class meant that more people could read. They learnt about politics from newspapers and many people became dissatisfied with their lack of rights. Trade Unions fought to improve wages and conditions for working people but found they needed new laws. When the Liberal and Conservative parties did not help enough the Labour Representation Committee was set up in 1900 to help get working-class men elected to parliament. In 1903 their 23 MPs decided to call themselves the Labour Party. However, they had little chance of making up a government until the vote was given to all adult men in 1918.

● *Votes for Women*

At the beginning of the nineteenth century women had very few rights. Even rich girls had little education as men thought their place was in the home. A woman was seen as her husband's property and he controlled her. Gradually, laws were passed to improve conditions, but many were still badly treated in 1898 as Mrs Pankhurst, who fought for votes for women, explains.

> **B** As registrar of births and deaths in a working class district . . . the women used to tell me their stories, dreadful stories some of them. I was shocked to be reminded over and over again how little respect there was in the world for women and children.
> . . . As a member of the school board I soon found that . . . men teachers received much higher wages, although many of the women had to teach sewing

and domestic science in addition to their regular class work. They received no extra pay and often spent part of their poor salaries to provide dinners for very poor children.

. . . Manchester Technical College . . . girls were kept out of bakery because the men's trade unions objected to their being educated for such skilled work. It was clear men regarded women as a servant class.

Emmeline Pankhurst, My Own Story, 1914.

Women had been trying to get parliament to give them the vote since 1867. Despite thousands of meetings and petitions with millions of signatures, the peaceful suffragist societies were getting nowhere. In 1903 Mrs Emmeline Pankhurst started the WSPU (Women's Social and Political Union) whose motto was 'Deeds not words' In the 1905 General Election campaign they went to meetings to ask MPs to say in public if they would give the women the vote. This is what happened when Annie Kenney asked this at the Manchester Free Trade Hall.

C The audience became a mob. They howled, they shouted and roared, shaking their fists fiercely at the woman who dared to ask her question at a man's meeting. Hands were lifted to drag her out of her chair but Christabel . . . helped ward off the mob, who struck and scratched at her until her sleeve was red with blood. Still the girls held together and shouted over and over: 'The question! The question! Answer the question!'

Emmeline Pankhurst, My Own Story, 1914.

Stewards threw the women out. When Annie and Christabel Pankhurst (Mrs Pankhurst's daughter), tried to speak to the crowds they were arrested. They refused to pay a fine and went to jail.

D A suffragette poster from around 1910.

This received lots of publicity and forced many men to start taking them seriously.

Women continued to explain why they should receive the vote as source D shows

Only by becoming more and more militant were the women able to get attention for their view, and marches on parliament became fairly common.

On 2 July 1909 Marion Wallace Dunlop went on hunger strike because she was treated like an ordinary criminal in jail. After 91 hours without food she was released. Naturally, other suffragettes did the same.

In September the Home Secretary ordered force feeding. Mary Leigh was one of the first suffragettes this happened to.

E The wardresses forced me on to the bed and the 2 doctors came in with them. While I was held down a nasal tube was inserted. It is two metres long with a funnel at the end. The end is put up one nostril . . . Great pain is felt. The drums of the ear seem to be bursting, a horrible pain in the throat and breast. The tube is pushed down 20 inches (50 cms) . . . The one holding the funnel end pours the liquid down, about a pint of milk, sometimes egg and milk are used . . . I was very sick on the first occasion after the tube was withdrawn.

The government argued it had to feed the women as it could not let them die or release them to commit more crime. Many people were horrified at the cruelty of the government.

After a general election, which showed the Liberals had lost a lot of support, there was a rest from the action as it looked as if the government might grant reform. When the government changed its mind the violence started again.

From March 1912 a campaign against property began, with the breaking of windows in the West End of London. Pillar boxes were set on fire, as were Ayr racecourse and buildings in places like Edinburgh and Aberdeen in 1913-14.

On 4 June 1913 Emily Wilding Davison was killed when she threw herself in front of the king's horse during the Derby. She thought men might take women more seriously if they showed they were willing to die for their cause.

The government did not want martyrs and in 1913 it passed the Prisoners' Temporary Discharge for Ill-Health Act which let them release hunger-strikers from prison and then re-arrest them when they were healthy again.

F The Suffragette view of the Temporary Discharge Act 1913.

The battle between government and women was still going on when war broke out with Germany in 1914. Women stopped the violence and their help in winning the war won the vote for some women over 30 in 1918 and all women over 21 in 1928.

1 **Men**
   a) How successful were working-class men in the period 1880-1914 in getting a say in governing Britain?
   b) When was the vote given to all adult men?

2 **Women and The Vote**
   For what reasons did women want the vote? (Sources B and D.)

3 How did some men react when women demanded the vote? (Read the text and source C.)

4 Use the headings below and draw a table showing women's struggle for the vote and how the government reacted to their methods. (The first and last ones have been done for you.)

Date	Methods of women	Government reaction
1867-1903	meetings, petitions	ignore
1914-18	war work	vote to some women

5 Look at sources D and F. Now choose one of the posters.
   a) What is it trying to say?
   b) How effective do you think it is? Explain your answer.

WOMEN'S RIGHTS

● ●

The list below shows how conditions for women changed during the nineteenth century.

1832 Women were not allowed to vote in parliamentary elections.

1834 Women were allowed to vote in town council elections.

1848 Queen's College for Women opened to give women an education equal to men.

1857 If her husband deserted her a woman could keep her own wages.

1860 The Nightingale School for Nurses was opened.

1870 Women could vote for the New School Boards.

1873 Girton, the first women's college, opened at Cambridge University.

1876 Medical Schools were allowed to take women students.

1880 Women could vote in county council elections.

1880 Married women could keep their own property.

1886 A woman could become the legal parent of her children if their father died.

1886 A husband who deserted his wife had to pay her maintenance.

1891 A husband could not imprison his wife.

1894 Women could be district and parish councillors.

The WSPU used stronger methods, campaigning against the Liberal Government of 1905-14. After Asquith, who was against women's suffrage, became Prime Minister in 1908, their chances seemed poor. Source H is from Mrs Pankhurst's account of Home Secretary, Herbert Gladstone's speech.

B. 60.

National Union of Women's Suffrage Societies,

14, GT. SMITH STREET, WESTMINSTER, LONDON, S.W.

LAW-ABIDING.   NON-PARTY.

President:—Mrs. HENRY FAWCETT, LL.D.

Colours—Red, White and Green.

Anti-Suffrage Arguments.

Anti-Suffragists say that the "The Voter, in giving a vote, pledges himself to uphold the consequences of his vote at all costs" and that "women are physically incapable of making this pledge."

What does this Mean?

When the issue at a General Election is PEACE or WAR, and a man votes for WAR, does he himself have to fight?

No!!

The men who fight are seldom qualified to vote, and the men who vote are never compelled to fight.

What is the Voters part in War?

He is called upon to PAY THE BILL.

Are Women Physically incapable of this?

Apparently NOT.

They are forced to pay in equal proportions with the men who alone have made the decision. Surely this is not fair! Since men and women are equally involved in the consequences, should not men and women equally have power to decide?

"But some matters discussed in the House of Commons concern men more than women."

True, but just as many concern women more than men.

Is not the Housing Problem a woman's question since

"Woman's Place is the Home?"

Are not EDUCATION, a Pure Milk Supply, and a Children's Charter questions for women, since

"The Woman's Business is to look after the Baby?"

Is not the Taxation of Food a woman's question since women are

"The Housekeepers of the Nation?"

Women claim votes, not because they are, or want to be, LIKE MEN, but because they are Different, and have somewhat different interests and different views. They want the vote as a tool, with which to do not Men's Work, but Women's Work, which men have left undone, or are trying unsuccessfully to do.

———— • • ————

LET THE WOMEN HELP!

"Two Heads are Better than one!!"

Published by the NATIONAL UNION OF WOMEN'S SUFFRAGE SOCIETIES,
14, Great Smith Street, S.W.: and
Printed by THE TEMPLAR PRINTING WORKS, 198, Edmund Street, Birmingham.

G Peaceful groups like the National Union of Women's Suffragist Societies (NUWSS) had put forward arguments like this.

H First academic discussion, then effective action, was the history of men's suffrage. (Men) know the necessity of demonstrating the greatness of their movement . . . they assembled in their tens of thousands all over the country. Of course, it is not to be expected that women can assemble in such masses, but power belongs to the masses, and through this power a government can be influenced.

Emmeline Pankhurst, My Own Story, 1914.

The women retaliated on 21 June 1907 with a march of 200,000 in Hyde Park. Asquith refused to change his mind and would not meet a deputation of women on 30 June. Police stopped the women marching on parliament.

THE GOVERNMENT'S VIEW

Some of the Liberal Ministers, such as Lloyd George and Winston Churchill, were sympathetic to the women's cause, but others were against them. The government had many other problems at home and abroad which demanded its attention. Ministers were also afraid that if they gave women householders the vote these middle-class women would vote Conservative, so making it harder for the Liberals to win elections. They therefore delayed a decision.

Then, when the violence was stepped up from 1910, the government was determined not to give in to force in case it encouraged other groups. The country was divided over the question of votes for women, whatever the government did would make it unpopular.

?

1 a) In what ways were women second-class citizens in the early nineteenth century?
   b) What political rights did they gain before 1900?
   c) Use sources B, D and G to explain why they claimed the right to vote.

d) Do you think source D or G is a more effective piece of propaganda? Explain your answer.

2 Describe the methods used by the WSPU.

3 How far does source H and the action of the government justify the militancy of the WSPU?

The Development of Trade Unions

Although Trade Union Acts of the 1870s gave legal rights to workers, including peaceful picketing, unions were still mainly made up of skilled workers who were better paid and difficult to replace.

Two important strikes in the 1880s changed this. In 1888 1,400 match girls from Bryant and May's match factories went on strike. They earned only about 4 shillings (20p) per week and suffered from 'phossy jaw', a disease where the phosphorus used for the match heads caused their gums to swell and their teeth to fall out. Annie Besant, a journalist, won sympathy for them and encouraged the public to boycott (not to buy) the company's goods. The campaign was so successful that the women won better wages and conditions. In 1889 the London dockers went on strike. They earned only 5d (2p) per hour and were hired to load and unload ships, and were often lucky to get two days' work per week. They demanded 6d an hour (the dockers' tanner), 8d (3p) for overtime and a minimum of 4 hours' work. The public was impressed by their good organisation and peaceful methods and a fund of nearly £100,000 was collected for them (£30,000 came from Australian dockers). They, too, won the strike.

I

British Trade Union Membership

Year	Membership
1888	750,000
1893	1,559,000
1900	2,002,000
1914	4,145,000
1920	8,347,000
1926	5,219,000
1928	4,806,000
1938	6,003,000
1948	9,632,000
1958	9,639,000
1968	10,049,000
1978	12,173,000

The success of these strikes led to the formation of 'new' unions for unskilled workers. Bricklayers' labourers, textile workers and builders' labourers all formed unions in 1889 and 1990.

Trade unions also seemed to gain some improvements after 1906, when Labour Party MPs helped pass laws to protect trade union funds.

From 1910 until 1914 trade was good and there was a series of strikes as workers tried to get their share of prosperity. Not all were successful but it looked as if things might change. In 1914 the Miners' Federation, National Federation of Transport Workers and National Union of Railwaymen formed a 'triple alliance' promising to help each other. The threat of a general strike was put aside with the start of the First World War in 1914.

In 1921 the miners called on their allies when the coalowners cut their wages. However, on 'Black' Friday, 15 April, the railwaymen and transport workers backed down. After a three month strike the miners had to accept lower wages. In 1925 employers wanted further wage cuts and this time the railwaymen and transport workers agreed not to move any coal when the miners went on strike. On 'Red' Friday, 31 July, the government promised a £24 million subsidy for 9 months while the Samuel Commission looked at the coal industry. The government also set up the Organisation for the Maintenance of Supplies (OMS), obtaining 100,000 volunteers to move essential goods if the strike took place.

The Royal Commission recommended reorganisation and an improvement in conditions, but also said wage cuts were necessary. A J Cooke, the miners' leader said, 'Not a penny off the pay, not a minute on the day.' On 1 May 1926 the miners went on strike. At midnight, on 3 May, the General Strike began with all transport, printing, dock, iron and steel workers being called out – around 3 million people.

The OMS managed to keep essential supplies going as the photographs show.

J Volunteers carried out essential services during the General Strike.

Most newspapers stopped publishing, although the government and unions each published their own newspaper. For many people BBC radio was their main source of news.

When the government offered discussions on 12 May the TUC called off the strike, partly because they did not have the money for a long strike. The miners felt betrayed and stayed out for seven months before hunger drove them back to work.

K In Kilsyth the lock-outs lasted for seven months and caused severe hardship. There were about 400 applications for parish relief each week, about one quarter of the town's ratepayers. This amounted to 10 shillings (50p) for the miner's wife and 3s 6d (17.5p) for each child or about one half of the miner's existing poor wage. 950 school children were given two free meals per day for six days each week, usually broth for four of the days and mince and potatoes for the other two. The Kilsyth Cooperative society . . . had 3,500 members, about three-quarters of whom came from mining families. Coop sales fell by 25 per cent during the lock-out.

James Hutchison, Weavers, Miners and the Open Book: A History of Kilsyth, 1986.

L I was almost four that summer of the General Strike but I remember going with my father to the bing so we could pick bits of coal to put on the fire. It was a good job the summer was good so I could run about in my bare feet with the other children. I can remember queuing with my father each day at the Salvation Army soup kitchen for a bowl of soup and a piece of bread.

An account by the son of an Airdrie miner.

?

1 a) What type of union was successful in the 1870s?
   b) Which two unions had successful strikes in 1888 and 1889?
   c) Why is it surprising they won?
   d) Explain why they were successful. (Think about publicity; public support.)
   e) What effect did this have on trade union membership? (Source I.) Explain why this happened.

2 a) Why did miners go on strike in 1926?
   b) Why did it become known as the 'General Strike'?

3 Use sources J, K and L to explain why it failed.

● *Contrasting Views of the General Strike*

These sources give two different views of the General Strike.

WONDERFUL RESPONSE TO THE CALL

General Council's Message : Stand Firm and Keep Order

The workers' response has exceeded all expectations. The first day of the great General Strike is over. They have manifested their determination and unity to the whole world. They have resolved that the attempt of the mineowners to starve three million men, women and children into submission shall not succeed.

All the essential industries and all the transport services have been brought to a standstill. The only exception is that the distribution of milk and food has been permitted to continue. The Trades Union General Council is not making war on the people. It is anxious that the ordinary members of the public shall not be penalised for the unpatriotic conduct of the mineowners and the Government.

Never have the workers responded with greater enthusiasm to the call of their leaders. The only difficulty that the General Council is experiencing, in fact, is in persuading those workers in the second line of defence to continue at work until the withdrawal of their labour may be needed.

M This is an article from *The British Worker*, which was published by the Trades Union Congress.

THE GREAT "HOLD-UP"

T.U.C. Threat to the Nation

STORY OF THE STRIKE

What is the General Strike about?

The Commission reported that 7 out of every 10 tons of coal are being produced at a loss. It also saw a revision of wages was needed to save the industry.

The Government accepted the Report. The Coal Owners accepted it. The miners refused to work a second longer or take a penny less even as a temporary measure to prevent ruin.

The Government strove night and day to secure an agreement. While negotiations were going on the Trade Union Council (without consulting the workers) issued notices for a General Strike which would paralyse transport, factories, public services, printing works, and the entire business of the Country.

The Government then put in force its plans for maintaining food and milk supplies. It called upon all loyal people to offer help.

As Mr Baldwin said, "the Government found itself challenged with an alternative Government." This alternative Government is a small group of Trade Union leaders. It represents only a small section of the people.

THE GOVERNMENT STANDS FOR THE PEOPLE- THE PEOPLE WILL STAND BY THE GOVERNMENT.

N This extract is from a handbill published by the Conservative Party.

?

1 What was surprising about the success of the strikes in the late 1880s?

2 Use source I and the text to explain the results of this success for the trade union movement.

3 a) What was the main reason for the General Strike of 1926?
   b) Study sources M and N and show how the government and trade unions differed in their views of the General Strike.

4 Use sources I, K and L to explain the results of the strike.

Role play
Find out more about the causes of the General Strike. Make up interviews with four people about their attitudes and reasons for being involved: a miner; a government minister; a coal owner, and an OMS volunteer.

● Education in Scotland

The Scottish School Pupil 1880-1930

In 1918 the school leaving age was raised to 14. This led to other changes.

O We propose that all children should be transferred, at the age of 11 or 12, from primary school to secondary schools, or to the senior departments of primary schools. Between the age of 11 and (if possible) 15, children should go to an 'academic' school, or a school where they can spend the last three or four years in a well-equipped and well-staffed modern school. There they will have practical work and realistic studies.

The Hadow Report, 1926.

By 1938, about 64 per cent of children over 11 were taught in separate senior classes, but teaching methods did not change very much. Janetta Bowie arrived in a Clydeside school in the 1930s to teach a class of 7-year-olds. She found on the teacher's desk, apart from the register

P only two other objects, a Bible and a strap. The headmaster measured out the cardboard for the primary modelling class to the last inch. There are fifty children. It seems strange that I should have fifty to teach when all the time there are teachers unemployed.

John Dewey, an American expert on education, said of Scottish schools:

Q There was a tiny handwork department in schools, often of a single room. In it basic woodwork was taught to a handful of boys, generally not bright enough to tackle the stiffer 'academic' subjects.

John Dewey, c.1937.

R This photograph gives some idea of a typical classroom at the beginning of the twentieth century.

?

1 Match up these beginnings and endings:

In 1918 the leaving age	separate schools for children over 12.
The Hadow Report wanted	were a Bible and strap.
Modern schools were to give	was raised to 14.
Common teaching aids	many as fifty
Class sizes were as	realistic and practical lessons.

2 Why is Janetta Bowie a good source for finding out about Scottish education at this time?

THE SCOTTISH UNIVERSITIES

In 1830 England had three universities; Oxford, Cambridge and London. At this time Scotland had four; St Andrews, Glasgow, Edinburgh and Aberdeen. In fact, Aberdeen had two separate universities; King's College, founded in 1495 and Marischall College, dating from 1593.

Unlike today, early universities offered only a few subjects. Glasgow University was founded for the study of knowledge 'in law, arts, and other lawful faculties'. It was not until the 1840s that other subjects such as medicine, science and engineering were generally available.

Universities were often situated in originally quiet areas of cities. Glasgow University was built in the High Street. But as towns expanded in the nineteenth century, conditions changed for the worse:

S Blackness, dirt, smoke, a selection of the countless smells of Glasgow, small airless crowded rooms thronged by scruffy youths make up a picture of the Old College of Glasgow.

M Lindsay, An Illustrated Guide to Glasgow, 1837.

In 1871 Glasgow University moved to a new site on Gilmorehill, on the western outskirts of the city. Between 1903-5 Marischall College in Aberdeen was rebuilt with a magnificent granite frontage.

T The impressive new buildings of Marischall College, Aberdeen.

These new buildings had much better facilities. In 1884 the Department of Chemistry in

Edinburgh moved into new accommodation that was described as 'palatial'.

Other changes occurred in the late nineteenth century. Universities gradually allowed the admission of women.

U This photograph shows Dr Mary Hannay, one of the first women medical graduates from Glasgow University, in 1897.

One thing that has perhaps not changed as much is the appearance and behaviour of students. These regulations were published by Glasgow University in the early nineteenth century on the occasion of a visit by two Austrian princes:

V
1 Students who have beards must shave them, and wash, as on Sundays.
2 All students must wear clean shirts.
3 Students of Theology must be combed, and wear black breeches and coats, and decent gowns, like ministers.
4 The juniors must not laugh, or make faces, when they see the foreigners.

M Lindsay, An Illustrated Guide to Glasgow, 1837.

Scotland's universities have always played an important role in research and learning. In Edinburgh, Brewster did important work in optics, inventing the kaleidoscope and improving the microscope. The importance of Aberdeen University has been described as follows:

W It gradually became the centre of learning for the whole of North-East Scotland and much of the North. To its classrooms came students from all over the area, to go out again as ministers, doctors, lawyers and scientists, to spread the influence and teaching of their professors, and to bring the lamp of learning to what had hitherto been an uneducated people.

H M McKenzie, Third Statistical Account.

?

1 Why do you think the learning of students improved in new buildings?

2 How do you account for the growth of new subjects in universities in the nineteenth century?

3 What does source V tell you about students at this time?

4 How important were Scotland's universities at this time?

13 ENTERTAINMENT FOR ALL

This period is often known as the 'Golden Age of the Music Hall'. But it is equally well known as the 'Golden Age' of the cinema.

The beginnings of the cinema lie outside Britain, with two Frenchmen, the Lumière brothers. Their flickering moving pictures created a sensation when they were shown here. Small 'picture houses' rapidly appeared in British cities.

As these moving pictures ('movies') were silent, with no soundtrack, they could easily be made in one country and shown in another. Many were made in Germany, but more were made in America. The sunny, cloudless days of California were ideal for making movies. By the 1930s, Hollywood, near Los Angeles, was the centre of the industry.

Improvements in cinema technology brought rapid improvements in the quality of films. Better cameras meant the films were clearer and less jerky than before. New and more daring stunts made stars like Charlie Chaplin, Buster Keaton and Harold Lloyd household names.

In 1926 'The Jazz Singer', starring Al Jolson, was made. It was the first picture with sound, and it was a sensation. Huge queues formed to see it.

Within a few years, silent pictures were dead; the last great one, Chaplin's 'City Lights', was made in 1930. Another major advance was colour, developed in the late 1930s.

The huge demand for the new films meant more and more cinemas, each with queues at its door.

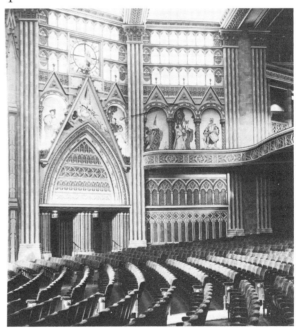

B Cinema interiors became more luxurious, like this one in Tooting in London.

A Crowds queue to see 'The Jazz Singer'.

1 Make a list of the improvements in cinema technology.

2 What evidence is there that cinemas became ever more popular?

POPULAR CULTURE FOR ALL

· ·

One of the main results of the boom in cinema audiences was the decline of the music hall.

The music hall was a variety theatre – it put on shows with singers, dancers, comedians, magicians, jugglers and so on. All the Scottish cities, and many of the larger towns, had their own music hall.

The most popular acts were usually comedians/singers, such as Will Fyffe, Harry Gordon and Harry Lauder. Many Scottish songs often thought to be traditional folk songs are actually music hall songs. 'I Belong To Glasgow' was written by Fyffe. Songs such as these had great appeal to the thousands of people who had flocked to the cities in the previous fifty years. They preserved some of the culture that they had left behind in the highlands and rural areas of the lowlands.

Some people resented this inferior copy of their culture, in particular, the mean Scotsman portrayed by Harry Lauder.

C Harry Lauder.

Others took a more practical line. Seeing that Scottish culture was already disappearing fast as people left the land, they began to collect traditional songs to preserve them forever. Most notable was the Aberdeenshire teacher Gavin Greig. His manuscripts formed one of the bases for the Scottish folk music revival of the 1960s.

Sport played a major part in Scottish culture. The Saturday afternoon football match played a fixed role in working-class life.

D This is part of the crowd waiting to get in to the 1937 League match between Aberdeen and Celtic. The same year a record crowd of 146,433 watched the same teams contest the Scottish Cup Final.

International matches, of both football and rugby, gave an outlet for the Scots' sense of national identity. Pride in playing for one's country enabled Scotland to establish a commanding lead in the football international series against England.

The importance of a rugby international against England is described here:

E The stand would be full of the sons of the Scottish race, every one both a patriot and an expert. In this way they released pent-up feelings, seeking to assert a Scottish identity, reviving for an afternoon the spirit of Bannockburn against the auld enemy.

S and O Checkland, Industry and Ethos (Scotland 1830-1914), *1984.*

?

1 What part did the music hall play in developing a Scottish culture?

2 What other factors helped to preserve Scottish culture?

3 What evidence is there of nationalist feelings in the Checklands' description of the rugby crowd (source E)?

4 Compare the picture of the football crowd with one today. What differences do you notice?

SECTION C

The Post-War Period

14 BRITAIN AFTER THE SECOND WORLD WAR

By Christmas 1945 the people of Britain had come through a terrible war lasting more than 5 years. Around 400,000 British people were killed in the war and half-a-million homes were destroyed. The war had also created many other problems which needed to be solved after 1945.

● *The Economy*

Britain was deeply in debt, the war having cost £1 million a day in 1939 and rising to £16 million daily by 1945. The country owed £35,000 million for war goods bought on credit.

It was important to return to a peace time economy and produce goods to sell abroad so that the debt could be paid off. However, coal production had dropped from 227 million tonnes in 1939 to 182 million tonnes in 1945 and the railways were overworked and needed huge sums spent on repairs. British trade and influence had been declining since after the First World War: how could the country recover when it had lost one-third of its merchant ships and exports were down 60 per cent from 1939?

● *Society*

People faced hardship as many foods were rationed. Certain foods such as bananas, oranges and ice cream had been unavailable since the start of the war. Clothes were rationed and coal was in short supply.

There was a shortage of 1.25 million houses and returning ex-servicemen needed jobs.

During the war the government had begun plans for peacetime, with the Beveridge Report of 1942 leading the way in dealing with poverty. Beveridge planned to give people 'social security' from the 'cradle to the grave'. The Labour Government of 1945-51 carried out the proposals and set up the Welfare State.

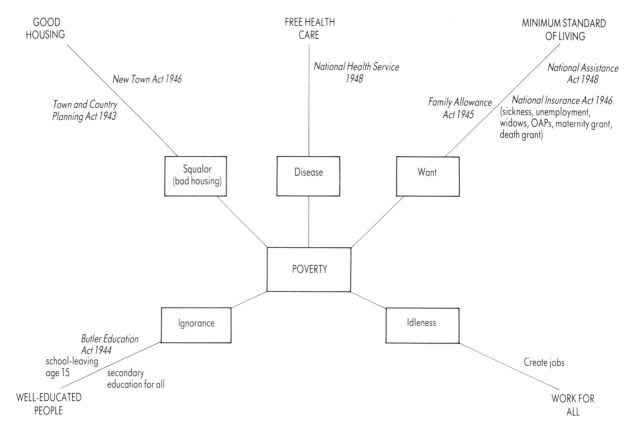

GOOD
HOUSING

FREE HEALTH
CARE

MINIMUM STANDARD
OF LIVING

New Town Act 1946

*National Health Service
1948*

*National Assistance
Act 1948*

*Town and Country
Planning Act 1943*

*Family Allowance
Act 1945*

*National Insurance Act 1946
(sickness, unemployment,
widows, OAPs, maternity grant,
death grant)*

Squalor
(bad housing)

Disease

Want

POVERTY

Ignorance

Idleness

*Butler Education
Act 1944*
school-leaving
age 15

*secondary
education for all*

Create jobs

WELL-EDUCATED
PEOPLE

WORK FOR
ALL

A How the government attempted to tackle the five aspects of poverty: disease, squalor, want, ignorance and idleness.

?

1 a) In what two ways had the Second World War put Britain in debt?

b) Why was it difficult to make goods in Britain to sell abroad? (Give three reasons.)

2 Give three ways life was hard for people at the end of the war.

3 Look at source A and make up a table showing how the government intended to tackle the five aspects of poverty. Leave four or five lines between each aspect. (As you work through the following chapters you can come back and fill in reforms.)

*P*OPULATION

Apart from a baby boom just after the war the birth rate in Britain has remained low as people have chosen to limit the size of their family. At the same time people are living longer, with the life expectancy for men being 69 in 1978 (46 in 1900) and 76 for women (52 in 1900).

B Percentage of Scottish population by age group from government figures.

	1951	1974	1991 (estimate)
Pre-school & school age	24.6	26.4	24.9
Working age	62.9	57.7	60.0
Retired	12.4	16.0	15.0

Since the war, governments have been concerned about the distribution of population. Britain averages around 770 people to the square mile with more than 80 per cent of the population living in urban areas. Concern over overcrowding and poor housing in our inner cities has led to the building of carefully planned New Towns.

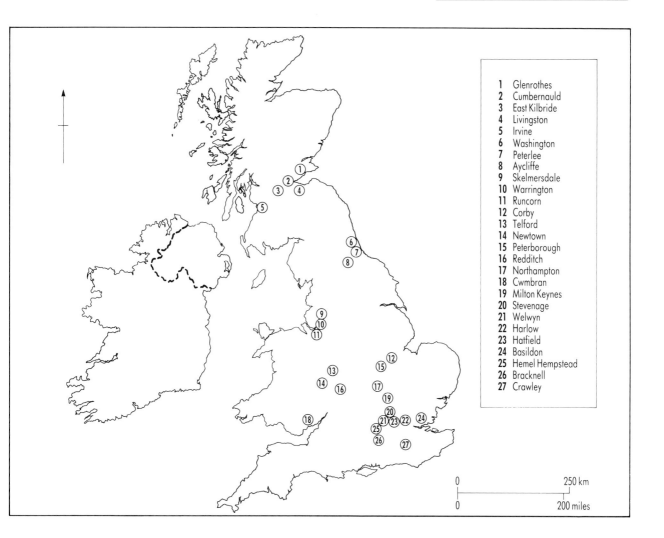

1	Glenrothes
2	Cumbernauld
3	East Kilbride
4	Livingston
5	Irvine
6	Washington
7	Peterlee
8	Aycliffe
9	Skelmersdale
10	Warrington
11	Runcorn
12	Corby
13	Telford
14	Newtown
15	Peterborough
16	Redditch
17	Northampton
18	Cwmbran
19	Milton Keynes
20	Stevenage
21	Welwyn
22	Harlow
23	Hatfield
24	Basildon
25	Hemel Hempstead
26	Bracknell
27	Crawley

0   250 km

0   200 miles

C   New Towns built in Britain since 1946.

Improved transport links have made it possible for people to commute considerable distances to work.

?

1   a) What economic problems faced Britain at the end of the Second World War?
    b) Why did she find it difficult to export goods?

2   Write a short paragraph describing the hardships faced by a returning soldier.

3   a) What five aspects contributing to poverty were identified in the Beveridge Report?
    b) What plans had the government made to deal with them by 1948?

Use sources A and B to answer the following:
a) What changes have taken place in the balance of population since 1951?
b) What services in the Welfare State would need more money spent on them as a result of these population changes?

5   Use a map of Britain to find out which cities would provide the population for the following New Towns.

New Town	City
East Kilbride	
Livingstone	
Aycliffe	
Warrington	
Cwmbran	
Basildon	

15

PEOPLE AT WORK

● *Shipbuilding*

The Second World War (1939-1945) brought an end to the troubles of the shipbuilding industry. The Clyde particularly gained from the need for warships. Shipyards in Dunbartonshire alone built two battleships, two aircraft carriers, three cruisers and 29 destroyers. Aberdeen yards built 114 ships, mainly landing craft, frigates and mine-sweepers.

Even when the war ended, the good times continued.

A There has never been a shortage of orders. 1951 was a record year. At the end of 1955 firms were claiming that their berths were fully booked for four years. Tankers were most common and they seem likely to play a large part for many years to come.

The Third Statistical Account for Dunbartonshire, 1959.

A warning was, however, given at this time.

B Output might well have been higher. It has been related in recent years to the supply of steel, the supply of man-power and the rate of work. This in turn is affected by rules about which workers do which jobs. Uncertain delivery dates and rising costs may affect the order books.

The Third Statistical Account for Dunbartonshire, 1959.

C This table shows how Britain's share of shipping launched in the world changed:

Year	% of ships launched
1945	50
1957	20
1971	5
1985	2

As a result of the loss of orders to foreign yards, many shipyards closed.

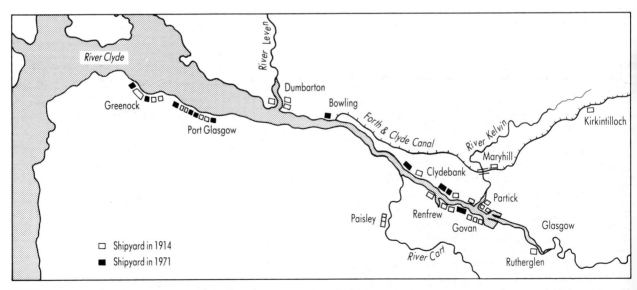

D This map compares the Clyde shipyards in 1914 and 1971.

Shipbuilding ended altogether in other areas, such as Dundee and Aberdeen. For workers in the industry the result was unemployment. Only yards which adopted modern technology, survived.

E Pictures like this one became a thing of the past on the Clyde, Tyne and Wear.

?

1 Describe how shipbuilding benefited during the Second World War.

2 What two things show that the 'good times' continued once the war ended? (Source A.)

3 What problems were shipyards facing in the 1950s?

4 What effects did the decline in shipbuilding have?

● *Shipbuilding's Problems after 1945*

British yards shared in the great post-war boom that lasted until 1955. Sandy Stephen came into his family shipbuilding firm on the Clyde at this time:

F Everything was very easy. People were able to make ends meet, we were able to make money. We could, within reason, ask what we liked for our ships. There were underlying problems, which while we were making money didn't really rear their ugly heads till later.

Quoted in *Overy and Pagnamenta*, All Our Working Days, 1984.

A world slump hit shipbuilding after 1955, but while foreign yards recovered afterwards, British yards did not. World output trebled in the next ten years, but British output remained static. In 1963, the Conservative Government announced special grants and credit schemes, but still yards closed. In 1965 the large, modernised Fairfields yard went bankrupt. The new Labour Government did two things; firstly the yard was partly taken over by the state, with public money pumped in and new management attempting to tackle the old problems of productivity, demarcation and manning levels by giving secure employment and better pay; and secondly it set up a government inquiry to find out the real causes of the industry's problems.

The Geddes Report (1966) listed shipbuilding's problems: management's attitudes to markets, men and money had been short term; individual firms were too small to deal effectively with customers and suppliers. It also said

G The past is very much alive in the minds of the workers in the industry and coupled with the general lack of confidence in the future of the industry it has bred a deep feeling of insecurity which is at the root of most of the demarcation disputes and practices in the industry which are commonly known as 'restrictive'.

The Geddes Report, 1966.

In one way government help made it even more difficult to deal with 'restrictive' practices.

H Financial assistance has had an adverse effect on industrial relations by encouraging the belief that public support [money] would be forthcoming whatever difficulties the companies got into.

The Commission on Industrial Relations, 1971.

The Conservative Government's policy of refusing aid to 'lame ducks' was ended by a 'work in' at the Upper Clyde yards in 1971. This led to a nationalisation of the shipbuilding industry by the next Labour Government in 1977. Even then the industry's troubles were not over. In 1977 British Shipbuilders employed 86,000 people but lost £106m; in 1982, under Mrs Thatcher, they employed only 66,000, but still lost £100m.

Opinions have been divided over the causes of this decline.

I There were plenty of good managers, have no doubt. But the atmosphere under which they had to work was demarcation and restrictive practices. I decided to pull my company out of building tankers, because they could build tankers on the continent with twenty per cent less man-hours than we could build them, purely because of British trade union practices.

Sir Leonard Redshaw, manager of Vickers' shipyards.

J I think one has to blame the management at that time for not taking more vigorous action. It's easy to blame the unions now, but the unions were not wholly to blame. With hindsight we should really have tackled all those demarcations vigorously, and they were capable of solution when things were good. But once times turned difficult, then its very hard to get things right.

Sandy Stephen, managing director of Alexander Stephen, the Govan shipbuilders, until 1966.

A Clydeside shop steward said:

K If they had given better job security, sick pay, pensions, better working conditions, and that was possible with the vast profits they made, then in my opinion they could have won the co-operation of the workers. But they felt that gaffers wore bowler hats,

and had the divine right to rule, and naturally if the management attitude is of that nature then the workers react in a not very positive manner.

Graham Day, a Canadian, was appointed Chairman of British Shipbuilders in 1983:

L British shipbuilding had not developed in plant terms, in work practice terms on the shop floor, in non-shipbuilding management-skill terms, in strategic planning terms, in marketing expertise, the way competitive industries in Sweden, Germany and certainly Japan had.

Graham Day.

1. How did government attitudes towards shipbuilding change between 1945 and the 1980s?

2. Did nationalisation solve shipbuilding's problems? Give reasons for your answer.

3. Study sources I, J, K and L. Which of them gives the most balanced account of the causes of the decline of British shipbuilding? Justify your answer.

4. Explain the main reasons for the decline of British shipbuilding after 1945.

Activities

Get into groups of about six. Each group represents a shipyard. Half of each group are its managers; the other half are its shop stewards, each representing a different one of its unions.

Your task is to persuade Graham Day (the teacher) that:
a) your yard should receive the £50m he has to invest, and;
b) yours should not be the yard he has to close!
(The teacher may wish to work this as a Balloon Night, with several rounds.)

*T*HE ENERGY INDUSTRY

● *Coal*

M This photograph shows George Scott, a miner, in 1947. He was born in 1872, and started work underground at the age of 12. The banner shows that the coal industry had just been nationalised; it was to be run for the benefit of the nation as a whole.

Mines were now encouraged to produce as much coal as possible; government money paid for much-needed investment.

N It didn't matter what it cost in overtime or machinery, as long as they could turn out the tonnage. I was in charge of one development and I wanted a conveyor, costing £38,000. 'Don't matter, you can have it'.

Walter Fox, mine manager.

At first the mines could not keep up with the needs of Britain's industries. But, by 1957, it was becoming difficult to sell coal, and stocks were growing at an alarming rate. This was the beginning of a long decline. As losses mounted, pits were closed. In 1957 there were 833 pits open; by 1970 there were only 293; and by 1987 a merc 108, of which two were in Scotland.

● *Electricity*

Employment in the electricity industry has fallen recently, from 201,000 in 1971 to 150,000 in 1986. In every other way the industry has expanded.

0 This table shows the amount of electricity produced, in millions of KiloWatt-hours:

1971	1976	1981	1986
213,732	235,756	242,106	261,181

In 1986 most of this electricity was made from coal (78 per cent), with 19 per cent from nuclear energy and 3 per cent from hydro-electric stations. In 1971, 88 per cent of electricity came from coal. Electricity output has needed to keep pace with the huge growth in demand from industry, and from domestic users – ourselves.

?

1 Some people have said that the period 1947-57 was a 'Golden Age' for mining. What evidence is there to support this?

2 What effect did the fall in the demand for coal have in the industry?

3 What reason can you find above for the fall in demand for coal?

4 With a partner, make a list of the things you each use electricity for in your homes. Then show how this explains the rise in demand for electricity.

● *Changes in the Electricity Industry*

No one could have foreseen the changes that have taken place in the energy situation since 1945. When Attlee's Labour Government nationalised the electricity industry in 1947, almost all electricity was made from coal, apart from the 2 or 3 per cent that came from the hydro-electric stations which had been built during the war, mainly in Scotland. Oil was scarce and expensive, though a few oil-fired stations were built in the 1950s. Even as late as 1973, the government's *Official Handbook: Britain 1973* said:

P The main primary sources of energy currently in Britain are coal, petroleum and, to a lesser extent, nuclear energy, natural gas and water power; secondary sources produced from these are electricity, town gas and coke.

Coal, mined within the country, represents 43 per cent of primary energy consumption, although the amount of coal used and its share of the total energy market has been falling. Oil on the other hand, virtually all imported, has expanded rapidly, its share of total energy consumption having risen from 20 per cent in 1958 to nearly 46 per cent in 1971. With the advent of nuclear power and North Sea natural gas Britain has moved from two fuels to four. A programme for nuclear power stations has been in progress since 1955 and nuclear power now provides a significant share of electricity supplies [9 per cent] although only 3 per cent of total energy requirements. The share of natural gas is expanding rapidly from the North Sea discoveries. Water-power resources are very small and cannot be developed much further.

Official Handbook: Britain 1973.

The equivalent passage from the 1986 *Official Handbook* said:

Q Britain has the largest energy resources of any country in the European Community and is a major world producer of oil, natural gas and coal. The other primary sources are nuclear power and some water power; secondary sources are electricity, coke and very small quantities of town gas. Since 1980 Britain has been self sufficient in energy as a result of the continued growth in offshore oil production, and self-sufficiency should be maintained for a number of years. Coal is the country's richest natural resource and is expected to maintain its role in meeting the country's energy needs. A major capital investment programme in the coal industry is in progress. Nuclear power provided about 20 per cent of the electricity available from the British public supply system in 1986, and this proportion is expected to increase.

Official Handbook: Britain 1986.

No one foresaw the development of North Sea oil. This transformed Britain's economy, and alone accounts for 6 per cent of Britain's wealth. It had a special impact on Aberdeen, North East Scotland, Orkney and Shetland. To these areas it brought thousands of jobs, higher wages and an end to migration southwards in search of a better life.

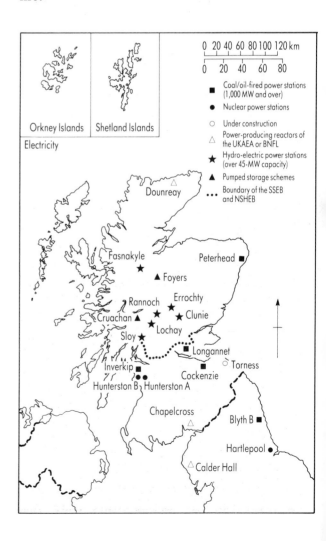

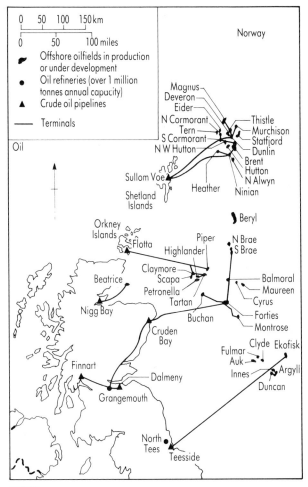

Oil

R The maps opposite and above show Britain's main sources of electricity and oil in 1988.

?

1 What attempts had British governments made to vary Britain's energy sources by 1971?

2 What similarities are there in Britain's energy position, as shown in the two extracts from the Official Handbooks? (Sources P and Q.)

3 How has Britain's economy been affected by the development of North Sea Oil?

Activity
Topic for class debate: 'The government's energy policy since 1945 has been a great success'.

THE GROWTH OF MASS PRODUCTION

• •

● *The Motor Car Industry*

S When World War Two started, car making stopped. The entire industry was put on to war work. The Castle Bromwich car factory alone provided seven out of each ten Spitfires made. The car makers' knowledge of mass production methods helped build aircraft at a speed the aircraft firms would never have been capable of.

Pagnamenta and Overy, All our Working Days, *1984.*

In wartime the government saw the advantages of mass production, just as businessmen had done before it; a large number of goods, of the same size, design, colour and quality could be produced cheaply and quickly; machinery could be used to turn out parts and workers specialised in one task only, which they could do quickly, and which earned them good wages. In 1914 Britain produced 34,000 cars; by 1930 output had risen to 180,000. In 1910 the cost of a Morris Cowley was £390; a much better model of the same car in 1930 cost £162.

Working conditions were not always pleasant. Hayden Evans left Wales to work in a car factory in Oxford:

T It was very frightening to start with. I had never been in a place where there was so much noise. The machine I was on was the equivalent of one of those hydraulic picks that they used to dig up the road.

Quoted in Pagnamenta and Overy.

Another problem was the speed of the assembly line. Tom Ward remembers:

 You had so much time for doing a job. If you were an ordinary time you got £2, and then you would have to go quicker and quicker to get more. And it would go up to time and a half, £3 a week. And when it got to double time they'd stop. No more. No faster. We could make about £5 a week. It was always good money in the motor trade if you could do the job.

Quoted in Pagnamenta and Overy.

Perhaps the worst thing about the car industry was the frequent spells of being laid off. Sometimes this happened because of production problems, like shortages of parts or breakdowns in the assembly line. More and more often it was because of strikes over wages or working conditions.

By the end of the 1960s the British car industry had a dreadful reputation for high prices, poor quality and late delivery. As a result of these problems, more people bought foreign cars. Some were made abroad, but in the 1980s foreign makers, especially the Japanese, started up factories of their own in Britain. One example is the Nissan factory near Newcastle. These factories use mass production methods, but output and quality are high. Disputes are almost unknown.

For British makers, the result has been a drop in output, redundancies and the closure of factories. Only in the 1980s, after the industry nearly collapsed, were the newest methods used.

❓

1 How did mass production methods help Britain's war effort?

2 Why are Hayden Evans and Tom Ward good sources of evidence for finding out about work in the car industry? (Sources T and U.)

3 In what ways has the car industry changed since 1945?

Activities
Discuss with a partner the advantages and disadvantages of mass production methods.
Then copy and complete these lists:

Advantages of mass production
1
2
3

Disadvantages of mass production
1
2
3

V This photograph shows computer controlled robots making Metros at Longbridge. Each of these robot lines replaced 70 car workers.

The Car Industry in Difficulties

There have been many explanations of why the British car industry ran into difficulties. There is no doubt that productivity (output per worker) was a major failing.

W

Productivity in major car-producing countries

	Britain	Germany	United States
1955	4	4	19
1976	5	8	28

X In the 1960's a number of problems came home to roost. Labour relations was only one of them though it became an alibi for others. Despite the full order books the profit levels of British companies had been low. Not enough had been ploughed back into new plant. With low investment, models that should have been replaced were allowed to run on past their time. This made them less attractive abroad, and more expensive.

Quoted in Pagnamenta and Overy.

By 1974 the situation was so serious that the government 'think tank', the Central Policy Review Staff, was called in to examine the problem. It concluded:

Y There is not the slightest chance of the British car industry becoming viable at any level of production if the present interruptions to production, reluctance to accept new methods of production and capital equipment, and readiness to accept sub-standard quality continue. These problems reflect prevailing attitudes of management and labour towards each other, towards productivity and towards work.

Quoted in Pagnamenta and Overy.

Government policies did not always help. To bring down unemployment figures in areas where older industries were in decline, the governments of the 1950s and 60s used a system of Industrial Development Certificates to force manufacturers to set up new plants there.

The plants which were set up this way were not, on the whole, successful. The Linwood plant, near Paisley closed after 20 years. A series of mergers left only four British car producers. A new tough style of management imposed new working practices and slashed the number of models; ten factories were closed and 70,000 jobs lost. Even so, British Leyland lost over £1,300 million in its five years under chairman Sir Michael Edwardes. Government money was needed to keep the industry alive. It survived and, in the 1980s, was returned to private hands under the privatisation programme of the Conservative Government.

Z The Linwood plant after closure. An auction of its machines is in process.

?

1 What evidence is there that British car makers failed to compete with foreign car producers?

2 What did Pagnamenta and Overy think were the reasons for the difficulties of the British car industry? (Source X.)

3 How far did the government's 'think tank' agree with them?

Activity
In small groups:

1 Make a list of the reasons for the problems of the car industry.

2 Each person takes one of these roles: Manager; Worker; Government representative.

Discuss which of you is most responsible for the difficulties of the industry.

WOMEN AT WORK

During the Second World War, women played an even greater part than they had done in the First World War. As well as taking the places in industry of men who had gone off to fight, the women in the armed services performed well. A US War Department booklet of 1942 said:

AA British women officers often give orders to men. The men obey smartly and know it is no shame. For British women have proved themselves in this war. They have stuck to their posts near burning ammunition dumps, delivered messages afoot after their motorcycles have been blasted from under them.

For those still in their 'peace-time' jobs, life also changed. Many found that rules of dress and behaviour were relaxed during wartime.

Many women remembered how the advances made during the First World War had been lost when peace returned. They were more determined that gains, both large and small, would not be lost again.

But, 25 years later, some women were disappointed with what they had achieved.

BB Women in our society are oppressed. In jobs we do full work for half pay, in the home we do unpaid work fulltime. Legally we often have only the status of children. We are brought up to feel inadequate, educated to narrower horizons than men.

Shrew magazine, 1971.

Changes in industry had helped to create more jobs open to women. Growing light industries, such as electronics, and service industries, such as banking, recruited large numbers of women.

CC A woman examining TV components in the Mitsubishi factory in Edinburgh.

But women were still more at the mercy of changes in the economy than men:

DD A growing number of women had gone out to work during the 1960's; by the late 1970's, with unemployment figures climbing upwards, they were encouraged to give up their jobs. One of Mrs Thatcher's ministers, Patrick Jenkin, said in 1979: 'If the Good Lord had intended us all having equal rights to go out to work, He wouldn't have created man and woman'.

F Wheen, The Sixties, 1982.

?

1   What shows that the US War Department thought British women had performed well during the war? (Source AA.)

2   How did women benefit from changes in industry after 1945?

3   What reasons does source BB give for women's lack of equality?

● *Women: Action Against Inequality*

As a result of pressure by women's groups, governments in the 1960s and 70s passed a series of acts aimed to improve the position of women. The most important of these were:

- 1970 Equal Pay Act: Men and women should be paid the same wage for doing the same work. [It came into force in 1975.]
- 1975 Sex Discrimination Act: Women were to get the same treatment, by law, as men in education, training, housing and employment.

It was hoped that these laws would change the inequality in earnings that women still suffered in 1975:

EE	Average earnings per week	
	Manual	**Non-Manual**
Men	£55.70	£68.40
Women	£31.10	£39.60

In 1986, however, an article in the *Guardian* reported that:

FF The latest New Earnings Survey figures for April, 1986, confirm adult male weekly earnings standing at £207 and women's at £137. In YTS girls are overwhelmingly grouped in clerical work and the retail and caring services. The pay differential between men and women (stays) . . . young men still have better opportunities for further training and promotion.

Maggy Meade-King in the Guardian, 1986.

The Equal Opportunities Commission had confirmed, the previous year, that women occupied only a fraction of the 'top' jobs:

GG	Male	Female
Judges, lawyers	45,000	8,000
Doctors	60,000	19,000
Accountants	204,000	23,000
Scientists, engineers	896,000	87,000
Lecturers	84,000	30,000

The Equal Opportunities Commission, 1985.

HH The Equal Opportunities Commission has tried to redress the situation by issuing posters like these from Northern Ireland.

Women still face yet another handicap in the struggle for equality. Madeleine Jones, in 1989, wrote:

II Today's women are little different from their medieval ancestors. They too might have two jobs – running a home and family as well as holding down a paid job in a factory, an office, in a shop, or in the professions. Men are rarely expected to do that.

Madeleine Jones, 1989.

?

1 What steps have been taken to improve the position of women at work since 1945?

2 How effective have these steps been? Justify your answer.

3 How valuable is Maggy Meade-King's article (source FF) for finding out about the problems faced by women at work in the 1980s? Give reasons for your answer.

4 Why in your opinion have women still not achieved equality with men at work?

Activity
Topic for class debate: 'Women will never achieve equality at work'.

16 TRANSPORT

● *The Car is King*

In the 50 years since the end of the Second World War, motor cars have become more and more popular. One reason for this is the continued improvement in technology.

A In the fifties and sixties the ideal was speed with style; in the seventies this was replaced by safety with economy. Research made cars more reliable. Improved designs increased speeds and improved fuel consumption.

Arthur Evans, The Motor Car, 1983.

B The results of these changes are shown in British small cars, such as the Morris Minor (1949), and the Austin Mini Metro (1980).

As cars and other road vehicles improved, they became more widely used. This table shows the increase of road vehicles in Britain since 1945:

C	1945	1955	1971	1986
Cars (& vans)	1.52	3.61	12.83	18.80
Motorcycles	0.70*	0.90*	1.00	1.10
Buses & taxis	0.04*	0.05*	0.07	0.10
Lorries	0.49	1.14	1.60	1.70
Total	3.11	6.15	15.50	21.70

(Figures in millions) * = Estimates

The growth of road traffic (5 per cent a year by 1986 and doubling every 14 years) has had several results. One is the increase in goods and people travelling by road. By 1986 82 per cent of passenger journeys were by car/taxi; 9 per cent by bus; 8 per cent by rail and less than 1 per cent by air. The figures for goods were similar, with water transport taking the place of buses.

?

1 In what three ways does Evans in source A say new technology has improved cars?

2 Study the two photographs of cars (source B). In what ways did the design of small cars improve after 1945?

3 What type of road vehicle grew most quickly in popularity after 1945? Give evidence to support your answer.

*T*HE MOTOR CAR: THE PROBLEMS OF POPULARITY

The problems of the growth of road traffic had been known for many years. By the 1960s they were becoming serious. In 1963 the Buchanan Report was published by the government. Its main recommendation was the separation of car and pedestrian traffic. One way this could be done was by building 'pedestrian precincts', where cars were banned and people could walk about freely. It also wanted the motorway network to be expanded considerably, and the flow of traffic in towns to be more controlled, for example, by one way streets.

D By 1971 the motorway network looked like this.

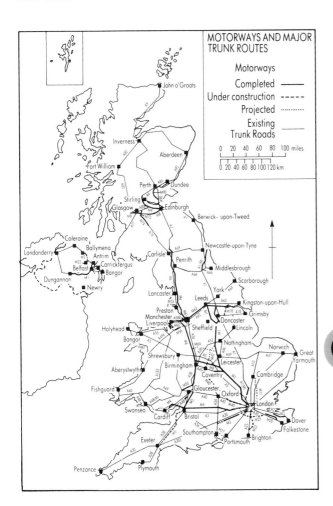

MOTORWAYS AND MAJOR TRUNK ROUTES

Motorways
Completed ——
Under construction ----
Projected ·········
Existing Trunk Roads

By this time government was committed to developing road transport, and motorways in particular.

E A large and steadily expanding road-building programme has been in progress since 1955. Public expenditure on new and improved roads in Great Britain is estimated at over £570m in 1972-3.

A government programme aims to complete by the early 1980's a comprehensive network of 3,500 miles of strategic trunk routes, including 2,000 miles of motorway, serving the main ports, airports and industrial centres and linking remote regions to the motorway network. In the interests of improving the environment, long-distance and in particular heavy goods traffic is being diverted from many towns and villages.

Official Handbook, 1973.

This policy was continued in the 1980s.

*R*AILWAYS: THE STRUGGLE FOR SURVIVAL

In 1947 the government nationalised the railways, realising that the Second World War had added to their problems of competing with the rising tide of road traffic. British Railways, later British Rail, found that public ownership did not solve their difficulties. Indeed, the lack of investment, especially under the Conservative government after 1979, made life even more difficult.

?

1 What solutions did the Buchanan Report recommend for transport problems?

2 To what extent had governments implemented these by 1971?

3 Has government policy since 1963 largely favoured road transport at the expense of the railways? Give reasons and evidence to support your answer.

17 HOME AND HEALTH

● *Housing*

In 1945 Britain needed 1,250,000 houses and the government planned to build 300,000 a year. By 1950 less than one million had been built. To help solve this problem £150 million was spent on prefabricated houses (prefabs) of corrugated iron and asbestos. They were only intended to last five years. In this account, a young girl describes her experience in Airdrie.

A Our single storey building was in the shape of a hollow rectangle with a gap at one corner. Around 40 families shared the drying greens and outside toilets. Our single-end was in the far corner. My parents' bed was in one of the recesses and my bed and my baby brother's cot was in the other. A wardrobe and sideboard took up the far wall. An armchair stood on each side of the fire and an oil-cloth covered the table and four chairs made the rest of the furniture. The iron sink was under the window and the gas cooker beside it. A gas light above the fire gave us light. We did not have enough points to put us at the top of the council housing list, but there was a gas leak which nearly killed us and we got emergency rehousing.

Our prefab had white walls and a front and side door. The electric light was such a novelty John and I had to be lifted up to switch it off and on. The kitchen had two sinks and the wringer could sit between them. The living room was as large as the single-end and beyond it was a lobby with the front door, two bedrooms and bathroom off it. Having an inside toilet and a real bath was a treat. We had our own front and back garden and a walk-in coal shed made of corrugated iron. We would have trouble with dampness and condensation in the ten years we lived there, but in 1952 when we moved in, it seemed like a palace.

B Prefabs in 1961.

Most of the houses built in the 1950s were council houses, but the 1960s and early 1970s saw a boom in private house building. As city slums were pulled down many people were moved to New Towns such as East Kilbride where tower blocks became more common. More than five million houses were built after 1945, but in 1976 one million homes still had no inside lavatory and 800,000 had no bath.

C The 15-storey Frazer River Tower in East Kilbride.

NEW TOWNS

• •

By 1971 there were 32 New Towns with a total population of 900,000. They cost £759 million, but were well planned with a Development Corporation to look after and plan each town, ensuring that all the necessary amenities were there for the people. As well as having a town centre each neighbourhood had shops, schools, and a community hall. Pedestrian safety was taken into account and there was plenty of space for children. The prosperity of the towns was ensured by ample encouragement for new industries.

One of the biggest changes in housing since 1945 has been in the number of people buying their own homes. This trend was increased in the early 1980s when the Conservative Government introduced legislation to allow council tenants to buy their homes. This policy has not pleased many councils as they have lost their best housing stock and do not have money to replace it.

D Changes in the Housing Market

	Scotland	England	South-east
Tenure (% 1988)			
Owner-occupied	45	67	68
Rented – local authority/ new town	46	23	21
Private rental or tied	6	8	8
Rented – housing association	3	3	3
New Dwellings (% change 1981-88)			
Private enterprise	+ 28	+ 63	+ 67
Housing associations	– 34	– 45	– 60
Local authorities etc	– 60	– 71	– 67
Market Value (% increase 1981-87)			
All housing stock	102	140	181

Secretary of State Malcolm Rifkind held a news conference to celebrate the latest returns from Scottish local authorities which show that sales of public sector houses have passed the 200,000 mark, bringing the level of Scottish owner occupation to 50.3 per cent.

Just over 20 per cent of the public sector stock, or one in five houses, has been sold leaving a total of 770,000 homes, the vast majority of which are eligible for sale to tenants.

The Convention of Scottish Local

?

1 Use source A and draw the table below comparing different aspects of the Airdrie girl's two houses. Add any other aspects you can compare.

	Single-End	Prefab
rooms	1	
light		electric
toilet		

2 Why did the girl think the prefab was 'like a palace'?

3 She wrote this account almost 35 years later. Do you think this makes her a good witness? Explain your answer.

4 What types of houses can you see in source C?

Authorities and the Scottish Council for Single Homeless accused the Government of neglecting the needs of the homeless.

Glasgow Herald, *August 1990.*

?

1 In what ways was a prefab better than a single-end?

2 Why was it not completely satisfactory?

3 Look at the sources about East Kilbride. Now write an advertisement to encourage families to move there.

4 What changes have taken place in housing tenure in Scotland in the 1980s?

5 **Group Work**
   Either prepare a questionnaire of at least 10 questions to investigate the housing of your classmates, or prepare a case for and against the buying of council houses.

● *Health*

Although 22 million workers were covered by the National Insurance scheme between the wars their wives and children were not. With a charge of 3s 6d (17.5p) for a home visit and extra for medicines it is not surprising the poor rarely saw a doctor. Dentists were only seen when a tooth needed to be extracted. Of the six million people who needed spectacles many had to make do with a 6d (2.5p) pair bought in Woolworths.

Following on from the Beveridge Report, the National Health Act 1946 planned:

● A completely free medical service for all – doctors, prescriptions, dentists, hospital etc
● All hospitals were nationalised
● 20 Regional Hospital Boards organised and ran hospitals
● Local authorities were responsible for ambulances, maternity and child welfare, home nursing and school medicals
● 138 separate Executive Councils dealt with doctors' pensions, chemists etc

E 'Dentist says if there are any more of you thinking of fitting one another up with National Health teeth for Christmas presents you've had it.'

This account tells what happened when the National Health Service started in July 1948.

F Surgeries were invaded like bargain basements. The 'family doctor' service was, at last, for everyone and they rushed to make use of it. Dentists were soon booked solid for many months ahead, and there was even a five months' wait for spectacles. Before long Bevan (the Health Minister) had to make a special appeal to the public to use the National Health Service sensibly. By the end of the first year 187 million prescriptions, 8,500,000 dental treatments and 5,500,000 pairs of glasses had been issued.

J Cootes, The Making of the Welfare State, 1966.

Ninety-five per cent of the population used the new service, with only 6,000 out of 240,000 hospital beds being kept for those who wanted to pay so they did not have to wait for treatment.

This service was the envy of the world but it was very expensive and by 1951 those who could afford it had to pay for prescription charges, part of their dental treatment and spectacles.

The National Health Service has had important successes. Killer diseases such as tuberculosis (TB) have been almost wiped out and people live longer.

	1931	1970
Men	58.4 years	68.6 years
Women	62.5 years	74.9 years

Different killer diseases such as cancer and heart disease have increased, but these may be partly our own fault as prosperity has led to an increase in smoking and unhealthy eating.

?

1 Which two groups of people were not covered by the National Insurance scheme before the war?

2 How did the National Health Act 1946 change this?

3 In what ways do sources E and F show you that the NHS (National Health Service) was needed?

4 Is source E or source F more useful in explaining how much the Health Service was needed? Explain your answer.

5 In what ways has the NHS been a success?

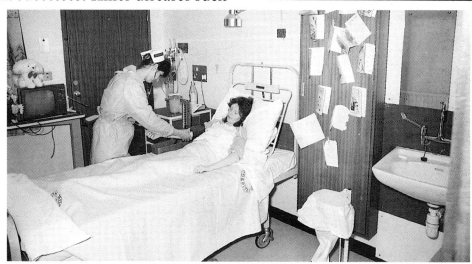

G An isolation ward in a present-day hospital.

RESULTS OF THE NHS

There is no doubt the NHS has made a difference to the health of children. For the years 1959-60 and 1960-1 Sighthill Health Centre, Edinburgh provided the following figures:

H Vaccination and Immunisation		
	1959-60	1960-61
smallpox	103	101
whooping cough	262	292
diptheria	156	193
polio	491	305

Free or cheap welfare foods supplied each week		
	1959-60	1960-1
tins of National Dried Milk	70	55
bottles of cod liver oil	18	21
packets of vitamins A & D	10	14
bottles of concentrated orange juice	124	131

Sighthill Health Centre, Edinburgh: Annual Report 1960-1.

Funding the NHS has always been a problem as only about 20 per cent of the money comes from insurance payments and the rest from general taxation. These government figures show how the cost of funding the NHS has increased:

Year	Cost (in millions of pounds)
1949	388
1958	700
1967	1,400
1971	2,270
1976	5,470
1981	11,944
1985	16,304

One of the reasons for the rising cost is that we have come to expect the best medical treatment, but the advances in medicine have also contributed, as a Wolverhampton surgeon reported in 1982.

I We can now save a limb crushed in a traffic accident but it may take four or more operations, five months in hospital and cost £20,000. A few years ago we would have cut the leg off and it would have cost £100.

The Sunday Times, 14 February 1982.

Longer life expectancy has also added to the cost of the NHS. The number of people over 75 years old in 1951 was 5.3 million, but by 1981 this had risen to 8.1 million. In the mid 1980s a man between the ages of 25 and 44 cost the NHS £82 a year, while someone over 75 cost £492.

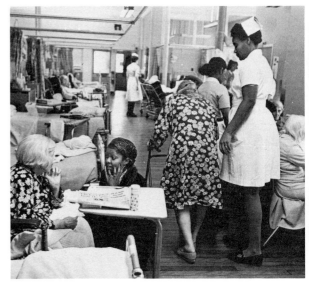

J Old people's ward in a London hospital.

It is, therefore, not surprising that people are constantly talking about a crisis in the NHS, with increasing waiting lists for hospital beds. By 1985 some four million people had turned to private medical insurance as a way of getting treatment quickly.

?

1 Write a paragraph explaining who needed a National Health Service and why.

2 What services did the NHS bring?

3 In what ways has the NHS helped keep babies and children healthy?

4 How successful do you think the NHS is? Give reasons.

5 How useful are sources I and J for explaining the problems of the NHS?

6 Find out what charges are made for the following NHS services: prescription, dental treatment, eye test and spectacles.

STANDARD OF LIVING AND POVERTY

*L*IFE IN THE WELFARE STATE

● *The Welfare State*

The idea of the 'Welfare State' is that the government should make sure that everyone in the country has a minimum standard of living. The plan for this was drawn up during the Second World War.

A This extract appeared in the *Daily Mirror*, 2 December 1942.

Beveridge tells how to

BANISH WANT

Cradle to grave plan **All pay – all benefit**

SIR WILLIAM BEVERIDGE'S Report, aimed at abolishing Want in Britain, is published today.

He calls his Plan for Social Security a revolution.

Here are his chief proposals:

All social insurance—unemployment, health, pensions— lumped into one weekly contribution for all citizens.

Cradle to the grave benefit for all including:

Free medical, dental, eyesight and hospital treatment;

Children's allowances

Increases in unemployment benefit; maternity grant; widow's benefit; separation and divorce provision;

Old age pensions.

Funeral grants

To work the scheme a new Minister of Social Security would open Security Offices within reach of every Citizen.

Between 1945-70 unemployment was around 2 per cent. At the same time there were cheap imports from the colonies and technological changes in industry meant goods were produced more cheaply. This meant most workers had money to buy luxuries. So great was the improvement that by 1959 Prime Minister Macmillan was telling the people 'You've never had it so good'. Even when unemployment started to rise there seemed to be an increasing demand for consumer goods to make life more comfortable.

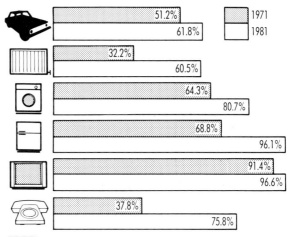

B The percentage of families owning certain household goods between 1952 and 1981.

Many of these goods were bought on H.P. – Hire Purchase – with families paying a certain amount each week over several years. By 1964 £1,094 million was owed on H.P. – £20 for every person in Britain.

By 1970 most people were only working a 40 hour week, with two or three weeks' paid holiday, and they had more time for leisure. The main hobby of older people was television, with more than half watching 15-25 hours per week.

There were 16 million licensed sets in 1970 (15,000 in 1947). People had a choice of three channels, with ITV introduced in 1955 and BBC2 in 1964. Colour programmes had appeared in 1967 and by 1970 half a million families had a colour set.

By 1977 there were 14.2 million cars on the road and many families were going abroad on package holidays.

?

1   What is meant by the 'welfare state'?

2   'From the Cradle to the Grave'. Make a table showing which benefits mentioned in source A were for children, women, adults, old people, everybody.

3   In what four ways did life for British people improve between 1945-70?

Group work
Make a list of new consumer goods which have become more common since 1981.
  Do a class survey to find out what percentage of people own them.

*T*HE BEVERIDGE WAY

The idea of state responsibility for the welfare of the people was something which had been growing since the Liberal Reforms of 1906-14, but the Beveridge Report was far more extensive than anything before.

Although the Welfare State is supposed to look after ALL citizens this does not mean everyone has the same standard of living. Most people have continued to improve their standard of living but some groups have fallen behind.

C   This cartoon shows Attlee, the Labour leader, driving a bus to 'civilisation'.

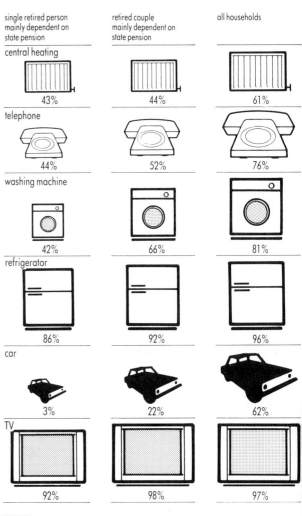

	single retired person mainly dependent on state pension	retired couple mainly dependent on state pension	all households
central heating	43%	44%	61%
telephone	44%	52%	76%
washing machine	42%	66%	81%
refrigerator	86%	92%	96%
car	3%	22%	62%
TV	92%	98%	97%

D   The ownership of household goods in 1981.

1 What parts of Beveridge's plans for the Welfare State were new and what parts were improvements on existing benefits?

2 Study source C. Is Low, the cartoonist, in favour of the reforms? Give reasons for your answer.

3 How far is it true to say there was a consumer revolution from 1945-81?

4 In what other ways have the lives of the British people improved since 1945?

● *Poverty Amid Plenty*

The Welfare State meant an end to *absolute poverty* – that is, having barely enough for food, shelter and clothing, but a survey of 1983 showed that over 7.5 million lived in *relative poverty* and lacked things that others took for granted.

E Standard of Living in 1983. The figures show the numbers of people (in millions) who have to go without 'necessities'.

Unemployment is one major cause of poverty.

F Number of unemployed in millions
Year	Millions
1965	0.3
1969	0.5
1974	0.6
1979	1.3
1984	3.1

Figures from Unemployment Gazette.

Source D shows that old-age pensioners tend to be worse off and this problem is likely to increase as more people live longer. In 1951 there were 5,468,000 people over 65 and this had grown to 7,306,000 by 1971, with the estimated number for 1991 as 8,988,000.

Low paid workers make the third group of poor people. They find it difficult to escape from 'the poverty trap' because if their wages increase, even by a small amount, their benefits go down.

In 1978 around 100,000 Scots were in one parent families (90 per cent female) and by 1981 1 million British families came into this category.

It is clear that relative poverty is not declining.

G The total of people in Scotland provided for by national assistance in 1961 was around 300,000 while our best estimate of the numbers now receiving supplementary benefit is around half a million, an increase over 16 years of about two thirds.

G. Norris, Economic Deprivation, 1978.

1 Use source E to describe ways in which the housing of the poor is unsatisfactory.

2 What four main groups make up the poor in Britain?

3 Use sources D, F and G to explain how poverty seems to have increased since the 1960s.

RELATIVE POVERTY

• •

The Supplementary Benefit level marks the official poverty line in Britain, but many people live below this level which is set so low that anyone whose income is 40 per cent higher is still living on the margins of poverty.

H   People must have an income which enables them to take part in the life of their community. They must be able to keep themselves reasonably fed, and well enough dressed to keep their self respect and attend interviews for jobs. Their homes must be reasonably warm; their children should not feel shamed by the quality of their clothing, the family must be able to visit relatives, read newspapers, retain their TV sets and their membership of trade unions and churches. And they must be able to live in a way which ensures that public officials, doctors, teachers, landlords and others treat them with the courtesy due to every member of the community.

Supplementary Benefit Commission Report, 1978.

Strathclyde Region published these figures in 1989.

I

Number of people receiving and number at or below Supplementary Benefit level (Strathclyde)

	1981	1986	1987	% change 1981-87
Number of recipients*	198,300	318,600	331,700	+ 67%
Number at or below SB level** Strathclyde				
– number	382,000	596,400	612,600	+ 60%
– % of population	16	25	26	+ 10% pts
Rest of Scotland				
– number	235,400	444,900	479,800	+ 93%
– % of population	9	16	17	+ 8% pts
Gt Britain				
– number	743,900	11,296,000	11,263,900	+ 52%
– % of population	14	20	20	+6% pts

* Including Housing Benefit Supplement.

** Including eligible non claimants and dependants.

Strathclyde Social Trends, number 2, October 1989.

The plight of one parent families is growing worse. Strathclyde's figures show that between 1981 and 1987 the percentage of one parent families in poverty rose from 45 per cent to 65 per cent. Many women cannot find well-paid jobs as they have to care for their children. They tend to live in poorer conditions, have less money to spend and are therefore in poverty.

J

Housing conditions of families with dependant children (Great Britain 1980-1 percentages)

	lone parents	couples
in rented accommodation	72	36
in flats/maisonettes	28	9
without central heating	48	33

General Household Survey, Social Security Statistics.

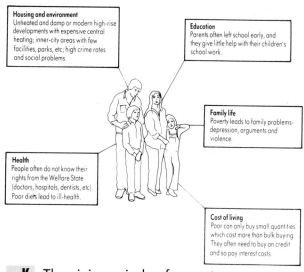

Housing and environment
Unheated and damp or modern high-rise developments with expensive central heating; inner-city areas with few facilities, parks, etc; high crime rates and social problems

Education
Parents often left school early, and they give little help with their children's school work.

Family life
Poverty leads to family problems- depression, arguments and violence.

Health
People often do not know their rights from the Welfare State (doctors, hospitals, dentists, etc). Poor diets lead to ill-health.

Cost of living
Poor can only buy small quantities which cost more than bulk buying. They often need to buy on credit and so pay interest costs.

K   The vicious circle of poverty.

?

1   How has our definition of poverty changed since the start of the century?

2   Which groups are most likely to live in poverty and why?

3   Use sources D and E to describe what it was like to be poor in the 1980s.

4   Has poverty declined or increased since 1970? Justify your answer with evidence from any of the sources.

NEW POLITICS – NEW PARTIES

● *The Vote for All*

The efforts of the ordinary people in the First World War earned the vote for all men aged 21 and over and women over 30. In 1928 this was extended to all adults. The voting age was not reduced to 18 until 1969.

● *Choosing an MP*

When some working men first gained the vote at the end of the nineteenth century they had to decide whether to vote for the Liberals or Conservatives. The rich landowners had most influence in the Conservative Party while industrialists and the middle class had most influence on the Liberals. Most working-class voters supported the Liberals but they were unhappy because the Liberals seemed to help the employers more often than the workers.

What the workers needed was a party of their own. In the 1880s William Morris and H. M. Hyndman sold over 100,000 copies of a book called *Socialism for All*. Its ideas have been summed up in this way.

A It pointed out that every year £300 million were paid as wages, but £1,000 million went to the capitalists (bosses) as rent, profit and interest. It called for the government to take over railways and land as a first step to taking over all industries and banks to nationalise them. The immediate task, though, was to build good houses for the workers, reduce their working day to eight hours, give work to the unemployed, and provide free education for all, with one free meal in school every day.

Hyman Shapiro, Keir Hardie and the Rise of the Labour Party, 1972.

Many trade unionists agreed with these ideas and in 1888 a Scottish miner, Keir Hardie, formed a Scottish Labour Party in Glasgow. He stood as a candidate for parliament in Mid-Lanark that year and made his view of working-class Liberal MPs clear in this speech.

B The man who poses as a Liberal, and yet refuses to support shorter working hours, an improvement in the homes of the people, . . . relief work for the unemployed and the return of land to its rightful owners, may call himself what he pleases, but he is an enemy and must be opposed.

Keir Hardie, 1888.

He did not win in 1888 but became MP for West Ham in London in 1892. The next year English and Scottish groups joined together to become the Independent Labour Party. In 1900 they joined with some trade union groups to become the Labour Representation Committee. A Scot from Lossiemouth, James Ramsay MacDonald, was made secretary. They aimed to put working men into the House of Commons and in the 1906 election the LRC won 29 seats.

The Liberals were quick to realise that these MPs, who now called themselves the Labour Party, would take votes from them. In the years before 1914 the Liberal government passed many reforms.

CAUSE AND EFFECT.

SOCIAL LEGISLATION
1906-1908
TRADE DISPUTES ACT
WORKMENS COMPENSATION ACT
SCHOOL-CHILDREN'S MEALS ACT
OLD AGE PENSIONS
UNEMPLOYED GRANT £300 000
MINERS EIGHT HOURS BILL

Keir Hardie: 'Look at that list, Mr. Bull—not one of them would have been passed if it hadn't been for our Labour Party!' (a cartoon of 1908).

C This cartoon of 1908 gives the Labour Party view of the Liberals' social reforms.

● *The Labour Party Since 1918*

Support for the Labour Party continued to grow after the First World War as the table below shows. The number of active members increased as did the number of voters. The Liberals lost support.

D

Year	Party Members	Votes	Seats	Events
1910	140,000	500,000	42	
1918	220,000	2,350,000	57	
1924	350,000	5,000,000	191	1st Labour Govt
1929	200,000	8,000,000	288	2nd Labour Govt
1945	300,000	11,500,000	394	Labour Govt (maj)

In 1924 the First Labour Government, under Ramsay MacDonald, did not have a majority and only lasted ten months. The disaster of the 1926 General Strike cut trade union membership from 8 to 5 million and showed that only parliament could improve conditions for the working class. The 1927 Trade Disputes Act said that trade unions could only give a part of members' subscriptions to the Labour Party if members asked in writing. This cut the Labour Party's income by 25 per cent.

In 1929 the Second Labour Government still had no majority and could not deal with the economic problems facing them. They resigned in 1931, though MacDonald stayed on as Prime Minister in a National Government with the Conservatives.

It was 1945 before the Third Labour Government came to power with a majority which let them pass the Beveridge Reforms which set up the Welfare State. Since then, Labour and Conservative have been the two main parties of government.

?

1 Rise of the Labour Party
   a) Which party did most workers vote for at the end of the nineteenth century?
   b) Use source B to explain why they were not happy with this party.

2 What were (a) the immediate tasks and (b) the long-term aims of socialists?

3 Why would Keir Hardie and workers support these ideas?

4 What effect did the Labour Party have on the Liberals? Use source C to explain your answer.

5 What is the evidence that the Labour Party became stronger after 1918? Use source D.

POLITICAL PARTIES SINCE 1945

. . . .

The coming of adult suffrage has led to political parties issuing a manifesto – a book showing the policies they support.

E

Area	Labour	Conservative
Economy	Plan development. Nationalise industries, profits to nation	Cut government spending. Let private industry get on and create wealth
Taxes	Take from rich to help less well-off	Keep taxes low, let people spend own money
Social Services	Free health and social services, low prescription charges	Encourage private medicine Encourage people to work
Education	Want comprehensive schools. End fee-paying schools	Keep selective and fee-paying schools
Trade Unions	Work with and strengthen unions	Reduce trade union powers

At general elections party members in each constituency help their candidate by going round the doors and spreading publicity.

Many people in the country do not support either of the major parties. In the 1980s the Liberal Party joined with the SDP (Social Democratic Party) – which had been formed in 1981 by right-wing Labour MPs to gain votes from those who thought that the Labour Party was going too far towards socialism and that the Conservatives were too right wing.

In Scotland and Wales, Nationalist Parties have appeared because they want to keep their own way of life and think British governments do not do enough for their areas. The SNP was formed in 1934 and won its first parliamentary seat in a by-election in Motherwell in 1945. In 1949 two million Scots signed a petition asking for Home Rule. The fortunes of the SNP declined during the prosperity of the 1950s and early 1960s but as unemployment increased so did its support, with Winnie Ewing winning a by-election in Hamilton in 1967.

F The seats won by each party in election in Scotland since 1970.

Year	Labour	Conservative	Liberal	SNP
1970	44	23	3	1
1974 (Feb)	40	21	3	7
1974 (Oct)	41	16	3	11
1979	44	22	3	2
1983	41	21	8	2
1987	50	10	9	3

The discovery of oil off Scotland's coast gave the SNP grounds for saying that Scotland could finance its own government from oil revenues. By the early 1970s the SNP was demanding independence. In 1973 a Royal Commission suggested a Scottish Assembly with limited control over housing, transport (not British Rail), law, local government and education. In 1974 official government figures revealed the value of the oil from taxation was £3 billion a year. The SNP cry 'Scotland's oil' was one many voters seemed to agree with.

In 1979 a referendum was held on the Assembly proposals. Only 62.9 per cent of people voted with 1,230,937 (51.6 per cent) in favour and 1,153,502 (48.4 per cent) against. However, the government had said beforehand that 40 per cent of all voters would need to approve of the changes and only 32.85 per cent had, so devolution was dropped for the time being.

G The percentage of votes for the SNP in recent elections and the number of seats they gained.

Year	Number of votes	% of votes	seats won
1970	306,802	11.4	1
1974 (Feb)	633,180	21.9	7
1974 (Oct)	839,617	30.4	11
1979	504,259	18.4	2
1983	332,045	11.8	2

In the 1983 election the SNP argued

H Whichever English party wins the election, regional aid will be redirected to the Midlands of England, to Scotland's disadvantage . . . Never has the need for an independent Scottish Parliament and a Scottish government been greater.

Only with our own Government will Scotland have the will and the resources to reverse our economic decline and end mass unemployment . . . to remove all nuclear weapons from our soil, . . . to tackle the appalling social conditions in which many of our people have to live.

The Scottish Nationalist Party, 1983.

Since 1983 the Labour manifesto has promised an Assembly with tax raising powers. When SNP candidate Jim Sillars won the Govan by-election in November 1988 its fortune seemed to be improving at the expense of the Labour Party.

I Jim Sillars with pop stars Pat Kane (left) and Craig and Charles Reid of the Proclaimers.

Trade unions, churches, prominent people and all parties, except the Conservatives, agreed to set up a Constitutional Convention to look at devolution. The SNP withdrew in February 1989 because it was offered only 8 per cent of the seats, which meant that Labour would dominate the Convention. To many people it looked as if the SNP was being obstructive but it believed that, as usual, it was being unfairly treated by the two major parties. The system of 'first pass the post' voting in British elections helps the major parties as shown by the 1983 General Election results.

J 1983 General Election results.

Party	Votes ('000)	No of MPs	Average vote per MP
Conservative	12,991	397	32,723
Labour	8,432	209	40,368
Liberal/SDP Alliance	7,775	23	338,043
Communist	12	0	–
Plaid Cymru (Welsh Nationalist Party)	125	2	62,500
SNP (Scottish Nationalist Party)	331	2	165,500

As Britain moves into the 1990s the role of the SNP and other parties remains an important issue.

?

Rise of the Labour Party

1 Explain fully why a new 'Labour' party was formed at the end of the nineteenth century.

2 What effect did it have on other political parties?

3 a) Describe the growth of the Labour Party between the wars.
b) Why was it unable to pass the reforms it promised?

Political Parties Since 1945

4 Use source E to explain which political party since 1945 might claim to be:
a) 'the party of free enterprise and choice'
b) 'the party of caring and equality'

5 Why has there been support for the Scottish Nationalist Party since 1945?

6 Is there any evidence to show that the SNP has forced the major parties to pay more attention to Scotland? You may use information from other chapters if you wish.

7 Why would source I be good propaganda for the SNP?

Class exercise
Hold a mock-election with candidates from the different parties putting forward their case.

20 LIFE AND CULTURE 1945-1990

The prosperity of the 1950s and 1960s put more money into the pockets of young people. A new youth culture appeared as the young spent money on music and clothes that appealed to them. For the first time music and fashion was aimed at teenagers.

At first, the main influences in music came from America, in the form of rock 'n' roll. In 1956 Bill Haley's film, Rock Around the Clock, caused teenagers to riot when it was shown in Britain. Soon, other American singers, such as Elvis Presley and Chuck Berry, had big followings. Only Cliff Richard and Tommy Steele became real British successes. This changed in 1963, when four lads from Liverpool, the Beatles, reached number 1 in the charts three times that year. The Beatles were incredibly popular and their music, hairstyles and clothes were quickly copied by their fans.

Later in the 1960s and 70s different groups of young people found their own special taste in music. 'Modernists', or mods, followed modern jazz; 'rockers' returned to old-style rock 'n' roll; hippies turned to flower power. Existing radio stations (the BBC) could not cope with the new demand for pop music. In 1960 the only pop music programme on BBC radio was 'Saturday Club'. Pirate radio stations, broadcasting from ships offshore, filled the gap.

A There was little doubt about the popularity of the Beatles. This photograph shows them returning to London after a tour of Scandinavia.

B This is 'Radio Scotland', anchored in the Forth in 1965.

107

These stations made their money from advertising. In 1967, the government reformed radio broadcasting. Radio One, a pop channel, was set up, with other channels for other ages and tastes. The pirate stations were closed down. Since then, commercial radio has moved back into broadcasting, and is now appealing to older age groups, with stations like Clyde Two and Capital Gold (London).

Clothes and fashion followed a similar pattern. Mods, hippies and others developed their own fashions.

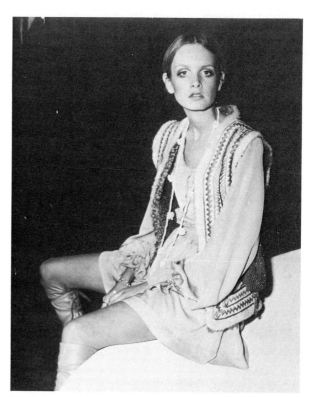

D Fashion models, like Twiggy, became national figures.

But, by the 1980s, fashions for all ages had become more alike, with one difference – older groups now copied teenage fashions.

C 'Flower power' followers in the late 1960s.

?

1 Complete this passage. The main change in popular music was the growing influence of _____. Singers like _____ _____ and _____ _____ became very popular. In the 1960s, this trend was reversed by four Liverpool lads called the _____. Their _____, _____ and _____ were copied. The growing demand for popular music led to the growth of _____ radio stations. As a result, in 1967 Radio _____ was set up. Since then many _____ radio stations playing popular music have appeared.

At the same time there were changes in _____ and _____. By the 1980s many people were copying _____ fashions.

2   What evidence is there that the popular culture of the 1960s was a 'youth culture'? Give at least two pieces of evidence to support your answer.

THE COMING OF TELEVISION

. . . .

As the working week got shorter, people had more time for leisure. Most of this was devoted to just one thing – television. Many people had one by the end of the 1950s. In 1961 75 per cent of families had one; by 1971 this had risen to over 90 per cent. People spent more and more time watching television; by 1982 the average person in Britain spent 20 hours each week watching it.

The effects were dramatic, as this table shows:

E	1959	1970
Cinema admissions	600m	225m
County cricket spectators	1.0m	0.1m
Football attendances	33m	25m

For the cinemas especially, television was a disaster. Half Britain's 3,400 cinemas closed in the 1960s; many of them became Bingo halls. Other forms of entertainment in competition with television fared better. In the 1930s the theatre just managed to survive, but after the Second World War it hit hard times. The audiences started to return in the 1970s, often attracted by the emergence of young writers, many of them Scots, like John McGrath. They wrote plays, often including songs, about issues that concerned their audiences; one example is the 'The Cheviot, the Stag, and the Black, Black Oil', about the exploitation of the Highlands.

Another reason for the revival in the stage in Scotland is the success of the Edinburgh Festival, first held in 1948. Although it is an international

F   These photographs show the Ritz Cinema in Edinburgh in the early 1980s.

festival, it has stimulated Scottish cultural life tremendously.

The most successful survivors have been the Scottish newspapers. Scotland has had long and distinguished service from its newspapers. In 1988, the Official Handbook said:

G   Scotland has six morning, six evening and three Sunday newspapers. The morning papers, with circulations of between 98,000 and 764,000, are The Scotsman, published in Edinburgh; the Glasgow Herald; the Daily Record; the Dundee Courier and Advertiser; the Aberdeen Press and Journal and the Scottish Daily Express (printed in

Manchester). There are evening papers for the four main cities, and for both Greenock and Paisley. The Sunday Papers are the *Sunday Mail*, the *Sunday Post* and the *Scottish Sunday Express*.

Weekly and local newspapers number 111, and there are 31 free weekly newspapers.

Official Handbook, 1988.

Since then, another Sunday newspaper, *Scotland on Sunday*, has carved a space in the 'quality' press. There have been, however, many casualties. Glasgow's *Evening Citizen* folded, while *The Scottish Daily News* and the *Sunday Standard* lasted for only a short while in the 1970s and 1980s respectively. On the other hand, the *Glasgow Herald* was founded as long ago as 1783.

The Scottish press has largely maintained its independence, and *The Scotsman* and the *Glasgow Herald* particularly have not been afraid to put the Scottish viewpoint. The others also put more local viewpoints and all give prominence to Scottish politics, sport, arts and events in a way that the London based 'national' press does not.

The importance of the Scottish press to the Scottish people can be judged from the *Sunday Post*, which is read by 85 per cent of Scottish adults – a world record for readership!

---

1 What effects did television have on other forms of entertainment?

2 What led to a revival of the Scottish theatre in the 1970s?

3 Why is the survival of the Scottish press important to anyone studying Scottish history in this period?

This editorial appeared in the *Glasgow Herald* in August 1990:

H There is a renewed interest in things Scottish, shown by an upsurge in publishing generally and by new books about Scottish history in particular. But this is accompanied everywhere by signs that our language is in disarray.

Rural speech, expressive and gramatically correct has receded as folk have migrated to the cities in an age of agricultural mechanisation. It is still to be found in corners of Aberdeenshire, Angus, Ayrshire, the Lothians and other counties.

The speech of urban industrial Scotland was always slipshod and grammatically imperfect, but it is this form which has shown the greatest powers of survival. The flowers have gone but the weeds remain. In commercial radio there is often found a curious mixture of slovenly habits and transatlantic influences. These are tendencies we deplore.

Glasgow Herald, 31 August 1990.

---

4 What have been the main influences on Scottish culture since 1945?

5 What is the attitude of the *Glasgow Herald* to these changes (source G)? Support your answer with as much evidence as you can.

INDEX